LADY OF SPAIN

Lady of Spain

❧

A life of Jane Dormer,
Duchess of Feria

Simon Courtauld

Anthony Eyre

MOUNT ORLEANS PRESS

Published in Great Britain in 2021
by Anthony Eyre, Mount Orleans Press
23 High Street, Cricklade SN6 6AP
www.anthonyeyre.com

Simon Courtauld has asserted his right to be
identified as the author of this work in accordance with
the Copyright, Designs and Patents Act 1988.

ISBN 978-1-912945-32-0

A CIP record for this book is available
from the British Library

Printed in the UK by
Short Run Press

TO JENNIE

Contents

List of Plates

Funerary monument to Sir William Dormer. (All Saints Church, Wing.)

Gomez Suárez de Figueroa y Córdoba, 5th Count and 1st Duke of Feria (*Historia o vero Vita di Elisabetta, Regina d'Inghilterr*a by Gregorio Leti, Amsterdam, 1693.)

Sir John Hawkins in 1581, aged 44. (National Maritime Museum.)

Portrait by Antonis Mor, listed perhaps incorrectly as 'Milora Dormer Inglesa, Duquesa de Feria'. (Prado, Madrid.)

Jane, Duchess of Feria, by Alonso Sanchez Coello, c1563. (The Royal English College, Valladolid.)

The widowed Duchess of Feria in the habit of a nun. (Private collection.)

Lady wearing a Cross, by Antonis Mor, 1567. (Prado, Madrid.)

Gomez Suárez de Figueroa y Cordoba, 3rd Duke of Feria. Detail from portrait by Vicente Carducho. (Prado, Madrid.)

A 17th c. view of Zafra by Israël Silvestre.

Queen Elizabeth's letter to the Duchess of Feria. (Public Record Office.)

Funerary monument to Catherine, Lady St John of Bletso. (Westminster Abbey.)

Lorenzo Suárez de Figueroa y Dormer, 2nd Duke of Feria. (Wikipedia.)

The tomb of Margaret Harrington. (The convent church of Santa Marina, Zafra.)

The Feria castle, Zafra, now a parador. (Simon Courtauld.)

Preface

HENRY CLIFFORD, who was a trusted member of the Duchess of Feria's household during the first decade of the 17th century and until her death, wrote an account of her life for the then Lord Dormer which was presented to him in 1643. The manuscript was transcribed in the 19th century, edited by the Revd Joseph Stevenson SJ and published by Burns and Oates in 1887. Much of it reads more like a eulogy by a devoted servant than a biography, and the chronology is not always reliable, but it has been a useful source for the facts of Jane's life.

My principal sources, from the National Archives, have been the various Calendars of State Papers—Domestic: Elizabeth, and Foreign: Spain, Simancas, the Vatican and Venice. I have also made use of the excellent website, British History Online. I have, however, followed the example of the distinguished Professor of English History, JE Neale, in his biography of Elizabeth I, and 'removed the elaborate scaffolding of documentary authority used in the construction of the book'. I have added occasional footnotes but no detailed source notes.

My grateful thanks are due to Professor Juan Carlos Rubio Masa for sharing his knowledge of the house of Feria; Professor Joanna Woodall for sharing her knowledge of the portraiture of Antonis Mor; Frances Kerner for transcribing Jane's letter to James I; Professor Javier Burrieza and Fr Peter Harris of the Royal English College, Valladolid; Fr Nicholas Schofield, Diocesan Archivist at Westminster; Jonathan Roche for his thesis on Catholic espionage in late-16th-century England; Lord Dormer and Emma Defries.

I have used the English spellings of the towns of Mechlin and Louvain which were current in the 16th century. (The French version of Mechlin was

Malines at that time.) Today the towns, which are in Belgium, are written as Mechelen and Leuven.

I refer to Jane's husband as Feria but, to avoid confusion, have referred to their son and grandson, the 2nd and 3rd Dukes of Feria, by their first names, Lorenzo and Gomez.

The European ducat and the English crown (five shillings) had similar values in the 16th century. One ducat would be worth around £100 today, so that the 3,000 ducats lent to Bassanio by Shylock in *The Merchant of Venice* would equate to more than £300,000 today.

Prologue

A SCHOOL PARTY was being taken round Burton Constable Hall in Yorkshire a few years ago. Among the rows of portraits in the long gallery, there was one in particular which impressed two girls who stopped to admire it.

'Isn't she lovely,' said one. 'A Tudor lady,' said the other. 'Like Queen Elizabeth.'

'No, not at all like Queen Elizabeth. She's just a lady.'

'I wish the others were here. They should all see her, because I'm sure she was a very special lady.'

She was called Jane Dormer, Duchess of Feria.

I

Two Monarchs

IN 1538, the year of Jane Dormer's birth, Henry VIII had nine years to live and would acquire three more wives. He had declared himself supreme head of the Church of England, breaking with Rome, and was seizing and selling the assets of the country's monasteries. William Tyndale had recently been burnt at the stake for publishing an English translation of the Bible, and within a few years the Council of Trent would usher in the Counter-Reformation. The Society of Jesus (Jesuits) was about to be founded.

Jane was brought up at a time of religious upheaval—her father was Catholic, her mother Protestant—which would only get worse over the course of her long life spent close to the centre of events, in England and Spain. She lived in a world of persecutions, inquisitions, executions, of espionage and deceit—and during several decades of conflict in Europe she made the acquaintance of the monarchs of England, Spain and Scotland.

The name of Dormer is thought to be taken from the French: D'Or Mer, or 'sea of gold'. True or not, the family apparently came to England from Normandy in the retinue of Edward the Confessor, who had fled from England during the tyranny of Harold Harefoot, son of Canute. Thomas was the first recorded Dormer, who helped to fund Edward's wars against the Danes, and Thomas's son William joined the Normans when his namesake, the Conqueror, invaded England. Dormers crop up again in the reigns of Edward III and Henry VI, in West Wycombe and Thame, where they became wealthy from wool. Two of the family, who were merchants of the Staple of Calais, are buried in St Mary's Church, Thame.

The Church of All Saints at Wing in Buckinghamshire has several grand monuments to the 16th-century Dormers. The first, commemorating Sir

Robert Dormer who died in 1552, is Roman in style, with a tomb chest garlanded by three skulls of oxen linked by swags of fruit and a canopy supported on fluted Corinthian columns. Sir Robert's son William shares a monument, incorporating two tombs, with his second wife Dorothy. A third monument, to the 1st Lord Dormer who died in 1616, has sculptures of his children on the base. (His grandson became the 1st Earl of Carnarvon.)

Sir Robert Dormer attended Henry VIII when Anne of Cleves arrived in England. He was made a Knight of the Shire and, in 1544, Henry appointed him vice-treasurer of his army in France. He remained in favour at court despite his unswerving loyalty to the Catholic church. However, Sir Robert's wife Jane Newdigate had a brother Sebastian who was less fortunate: having been a member of Henry's Privy Chamber and disapproving of the King's 'lustful appetites', he entered the London Charterhouse as a Carthusian monk. Here he gained a reputation as a classical scholar and met Thomas More, who regularly attended Mass at the Charterhouse. Newdigate refused to accept the King's assumption of supremacy over the Pope, was arrested for treason and subsequently hanged, drawn and quartered at Tyburn. It was said that Henry, in disguise, visited him twice in prison but was unable to persuade him to recant. More was executed three weeks later.

An inscription on a brass plate in All Saints Church records that Robert's son William's first wife was Mary, daughter of Sir William Sidney, and that they had two daughters. The younger was Jane who 'maryed unto Dun Gomis Swaris de Figueria Duke de Feria &c in Spayne'—or, as his name would be more generally written, Don Gomez Suarez de Figueroa, Count of Feria (the dukedom came later, in 1567).

During the 16th century the Dormers lived for a while at Eythrope, near Aylesbury, and it was here that Jane Dormer was born on 6th January 1538. The Dissolution of the Monasteries was taking place, and with Sir Robert's patronage the organ at Woburn Abbey, also a window and some ornaments, were removed and installed in the church at Wing. Unfortunately there are no records of Jane's baptism or of her early childhood in Buckinghamshire: Eythrope was demolished and rebuilt in the 19th century by the Rothschild family, who also greatly extended another Dormer residence, Ascott, and incorporated both properties into the Waddesdon estate. Another branch

Funerary monument to Jane's father Sir William Dormer, All Saints Church, Wing.

of the Dormer family also owned land in Buckinghamshire and a house, Tythrop Park near Aylesbury, which may have been built by Sir John Dormer, grandson of Sir Michael Dormer, who had been Mayor of London in 1541. A portrait of Anna Sophia Dormer, wife of the Lord Dormer who became Earl of Carnarvon, hangs at Tythrop today.

Jane was only four when her mother died and she went to live with her grandmother Lady (Jane) Dormer. Her maternal grandfather, Sir William Sidney, had fought at the Battle of Flodden and accompanied Henry VIII to the Field of the Cloth of Gold before he was made tutor and steward of the household to Henry's infant son Edward, born in October 1537. Sir William's son Henry (Jane's uncle) acted as one of Edward's companions; and it was unsurprising, in view of their ages (Jane was only three months younger than Edward) and despite her Catholic upbringing, that she was also invited to become the prince's playmate in the years before he became king. Jane would spend much of her time in Hertfordshire, at the royal residences of Hunsdon, near Ware, and Ashridge, near Berkhamsted, a former monastery converted by Henry. (Both houses have been rebuilt and today are listed Grade I. Elizabeth lived at Ashridge during Mary's reign before she was detained in the Tower.) The two children clearly got on well, often playing, singing and dancing together. He would call her 'My Jane' and she would later describe Edward as 'a marvellous sweet child, of very mild and generous condition'. The prince reportedly said one day, after beating her at cards: 'Now your king is gone, Jane, I shall be good enough for you.'

Although the Dormer and Sidney families were on opposite sides of the religious divide, good relations were maintained and their connections with the royal family were such as to enable them to survive the upheavals on the throne taking place in the years between Henry's break with Rome and the accession of Elizabeth. Jane's father, Sir William Dormer, was a member of Parliament towards the end of Henry's reign. Before his marriage in 1535, a rakish and unprincipled figure, Sir Francis Bryan, tried to persuade Dormer to marry his cousin Jane Seymour (she married Henry VIII in 1536). Dormer may have turned her down because his mother had already found him 'a virtuous gentlewoman answerable in quality'—Mary Sidney—or because the Seymours were not thought wealthy enough. Bryan was related to three of Henry's wives—Anne Boleyn, Jane Seymour and Catherine Howard—and was given the nickname of The Vicar of Hell by Thomas Cromwell. He schemed with Cromwell to bring about Boleyn's downfall; when Cromwell fell from power, Bryan kept out of the way and, as a notorious trimmer, regained the King's favour after Cromwell's demise.

The Catholic Sir William Dormer kept out of the royal limelight during

Edward's reign, but when Mary succeeded to the throne she made him a Knight of the Bath and Keeper of the Queen's Hawks in recognition of his support against the Duke of Northumberland, who had manoeuvred his daughter-in-law Lady Jane Grey on to the throne when Edward died. Dormer had married again but the conflict of loyalty to his first wife Mary's family may have given him pause. The Sidneys not only embraced the reformed Protestant church but there was a direct family link to the Duke of Northumberland through his daughter who married Henry Sidney, Mary Dormer's brother and Edward's childhood friend who was at the young king's bedside when he died.

The devious Duke of Northumberland was John Dudley, Earl of Warwick, when the nine-year-old Edward succeeded to the throne. The Council appointed for Edward's minority was headed by his uncle, Edward Seymour, Earl of Hertford, who became Duke of Somerset, taking the title of Lord Protector. After a couple of years the Council removed him, he was sent to the Tower and was replaced as leader of the Council by Dudley, who awarded himself the dukedom of Northumberland. Somerset was released, then rearrested, convicted of felony and executed in 1552. (His widow married Francis Newdigate, a nephew of Jane Dormer's grandmother.)

During the brief years of Edward's reign Protestantism took over. Images were removed from churches; the table replaced the altar; masses for the dead were abolished; the communion service was spoken, sermons given and the Bible read, in English; and the Book of Common Prayer was brought into use. Young Jane Dormer, who didn't enter her teenage years until 1551, found all this confusing and disturbing. She remained fond of Edward, her childhood companion, but her strongest influence was her staunchly Catholic paternal grandmother with whom she was living most of the time. Adding to her confusion, Jane's great-uncle by marriage, the Duke of Northumberland, was the effective ruler of the country, forcing religious reform and giving Protestant preachers free rein. However, two of her Sidney aunts had been in Princess Mary's service before her father's death. They refused to leave her when Henry wanted them to serve his sixth wife and both remained with Mary until they died. Employment with Mary was said to be 'the only harbour for honourable young gentlewomen, given any way to piety and devotion. It was the true school of virtuous demeanour, befitting the education that ought to be in noble damsels.' The household was characterised as a 'chaste school', which referred not only to its sexual purity but, in Middle English, to the restraint and discipline exercised by Mary. Jane was already reading the Office of Our Blessed Lady in Latin when she entered Princess Mary's service She was barely ten years old and at an age when the piety of her mistress would be imprinted on her for the rest of her life.

So Jane now agreed, with her grandmother's encouragement, to join Mary's household as one of her ladies of the bedchamber. Although Jane may have been perceived as having changed sides, this was not as embarrassing as it might have appeared. Edward and his half-sister Mary (older by 21 years) were on good terms: she showed 'great affection and sisterly care of him', he 'took special content' in her company and to an extent looked up to her as counsellor and surrogate mother. When she visited him 'the young king would burst forth in tears, grieving matters could not be according to her will and desire. When she was to take leave, he seemed to part from her with sorrow; he kissed her, he called for some jewel to present her, he complained that they gave him no better to give her.' Edward also promised to keep secret anything she confided to him, and he did not intervene to stop her regular celebration of Mass in her chapel. However, when this came to the attention of the Council, Edward was prevailed on to write a letter demanding that Mary conform to the Anglican liturgy. When she resisted, she told her half-brother that she offered her body to his majesty's service and her soul to God; and she asked him to 'take her life rather than the old religion, in which she desired to live and die'. The 13-year-old king was not going to insist on such a sacrifice; and when, on the following day, the imperial ambassador delivered a message from his master Charles V that if Mary were denied the Mass he would declare war on England, the Council had to give way. But Edward hardened his heart against Mary, relations between them deteriorated, and officers of her household were arrested. Two years passed before Edward and Mary met again, shortly before he died.

Northumberland had arranged for his son Guildford to marry Lady Jane Grey in May 1553 and had her proclaimed queen in the Tower of London after Edward's death at the beginning of July (they were the same age, both born in October 1537). But her reign was no more than a nine-day wonder: Mary withdrew to Suffolk, Northumberland went after her with his forces and sent six ships to lie off the Norfolk coast and arrest her if she tried to escape to Flanders. But the crews deserted to Mary and when Northumberland reached Cambridge he learnt that the Council, realising support for Mary was growing daily all over southern England, had no hesitation in abandoning poor Jane Grey and her deluded father-in-law. Northumberland was arrested and executed a month later. Lady Jane Grey and her husband lived on in the Tower for another six months before Mary was persuaded that they should not be spared.

During the days when Lady Jane Grey was nominally queen, Jane Dormer's father Sir William took it upon himself to declare Buckinghamshire for Mary. To achieve this he went to Aylesbury with a number of supporters to confront the Earl of Bedford, who had proclaimed Lady Jane as queen. 'My Lord, we cannot hear of any queen but the Lady Mary,' Sir William told him; 'and he that presumes publicly to name any other shall do it to his cost.' Bedford was 'affrighted' and retired.

Jane Dormer, meanwhile, was in attendance on Mary as she left Hoddesdon in Hertfordshire on hearing of Edward's death and rode through the night towards Kenninghall in Norfolk, some 80 miles away. When Lady Jane Grey was proclaimed queen three days later, Mary rode on to the well-fortified Framlingham Castle, whose walls were 40 feet high and crowned with 13 square towers. Arriving exhausted on 13th July, Mary's spirits were soon lifted when large numbers of knights and peasants, from all over Norfolk and Suffolk, began to rally to her cause. Over the next six days several thousand, including the sailors who had mutinied, declared their support for Mary, making up a formidable army to set against Northumberland. During that nerve-racking week, Mary was writing to the emperor's envoys to enlist their active support but didn't know that her cousin Charles V had in effect abandoned her cause and that his ambassadors had told him that 'we believe that my lady will be in [Northumberland's] hands in four days'. Nor did she know what was happening in London. On the day that she rode out of the castle to inspect her troops and await Northumberland's attack, he gave up without a fight.

During the previous days, however, she had had time within the castle walls to consider her fate. One may imagine that she and Jane Dormer would have occupied some of their enforced inactivity in doing needlework.

Jane was known to be proficient at stitching and embroidery, a skill with which Mary was also familiar, inherited from her Spanish mother and her aunt. When Catherine of Aragon came to England in 1501 to marry Prince Arthur, she brought garments embroidered with black thread (blackwork) which came to be known as Spanish work and was popular in England throughout the 16th century. Portraits of Queen Elizabeth show her wearing sleeves of blackwork. Another variety of embroidery was known as sampler stitching or needlework. A collection of 50 samplers were listed in an inventory of the possessions of Catherine's elder sister Juana, mother of Charles V, who may have had little else to do during the last 45 years of her life when she was confined to a convent. Mary was confined to her Suffolk castle for a week. News of Northumberland's surrender reached Framlingham a couple of days after Mary was proclaimed queen in London, but she waited until she was assured that all rebels had been arrested before entering the capital on 3rd August. Her coronation followed at the end of September. Princess Elizabeth and Anne of Cleves rode together in the procession, and among Mary's nine gentlewomen in attendance were Jane and a Miss Sidney, who may have been one of Jane's aunts, possibly Frances who, like her brother Henry, served both Mary and Elizabeth. Frances married the Earl of Sussex, who preceded Henry Sidney as Lord Deputy of Ireland in Elizabeth's reign, and after whom Sidney Sussex College in Cambridge was named.

Apart from Matilda, Henry I's daughter and sole legitimate heir, who was never formally declared queen during the anarchy of Stephen's reign, Mary was the first queen to sit on the throne of England in her own right. It was unthinkable that she should reign alone—her Spanish grandmother Isabella had been Queen Regnant, though in partnership with her husband Ferdinand—and suitors lost no time in presenting themselves. Most notable was Edward Courtenay, Edward IV's great-grandson and a second cousin to Mary. He had been imprisoned with his parents by Henry VIII and was not released until Mary became queen. She promptly made him Earl of Devon and he carried the sword of state at her coronation. No doubt he was encouraged to think that marriage to Mary was on the cards—after all, he was of the blood royal—but he made the mistake of also pressing his suit elsewhere. He not only flirted with the Queen's lady-in-waiting Jane Dormer, but began to pay court to her half-sister Elizabeth.

At this time, rumour was spreading that a marriage was contemplated between Mary and Prince Philip of Spain, son of the Emperor Charles V. Opposition to an Anglo-Spanish alliance was fuelled by money and propaganda from France and led to a short-lived rebellion orchestrated by one Thomas Wyatt in January 1554. The idea was that Elizabeth would replace Mary on the throne and marry Lord Devon. The extent of their involvement in such a plot was never proved, but it put paid to Devon's chances of marrying either sister, and he was exiled to the Venetian Republic, where he died shortly afterwards.

As soon as Mary became queen and was encouraged to choose a husband, her immediate inclination was towards a Spanish match. She was, after all, half-Spanish by birth, and possibly more than half-Spanish by outlook and attitude. During her childhood, and while her mother Catherine of Aragon was still queen, Mary had a Spanish tutor, Juan Luis Vives, who guided her in matters of learning and culture. He was a friend of Erasmus, also Wolsey and More, he wrote *Instructions of a Christian Woman* for his royal pupil and instructed her until she was 12 years old. It was hardly surprising, therefore, that she should turn to her cousin Charles V for advice once she had ascended the throne. Having initially doubted whether she could oust Lady Jane Grey, he and his ambassador in London, Simon Renard, moved quickly to arrange a marriage and therefore a political union against France.

In her letters to Charles, to whom she had been nominally betrothed at the age of six, Mary signed herself 'your loving sister, cousin, daughter and ally for ever', though no doubt without any hope or expectation of marrying a man who was now in his mid-50s. But there was the Emperor's son and heir, Philip, who was told by his father he must do his duty. England would return to the Catholic fold, with effectively a Spanish guarantee, and France's influence in Scotland could be marginalised. The imperial envoy, Simon Renard, was already discussing the desirability of the marriage with Mary in September 1553, and the following month he proposed to the Queen on the prince's behalf. She gave her formal acceptance two weeks later.

Mary was 38 years old, 11 years Philip's senior, prompting the Venetian ambassador to comment rather bitchily that 'were not her age on the decline, she might be called handsome rather than the contrary'. Philip must have looked forward to his second marriage with less than wholehearted enthusiasm; he had hoped that his father would marry her himself. But he bit the bullet and made preparations to sail to England.

When a portrait of Philip, by Titian, was sent to England and arrived at Hampton Court, Mary was immediately struck by the face of the man she was to marry. In Philippa Gregory's novel, *The Queen's Fool*, she has Jane Dormer presenting the painting to Mary for her inspection. '"My God, Jane, this is a man," she whispered. "He's very... pleasing." "What dark eyes he has," Jane pointed out. "Yes," the Queen breathed.' Unfortunately, Philip was not similarly enamoured of his wife-to-be. The historian J A Froude has written of 'the unhappy queen, unloved, unlovable, yet with her parched heart thirsting for affection, was flinging herself upon a breast to which an iceberg was warm; upon a man to whom love was an unmeaning word, except as the most brutal of passions.' Sir Charles Petrie put it succinctly in his biography, *Philip II of Spain*: 'The tragedy was that Mary undoubtedly fell in love with Philip, and there is nothing more boring to a young man than the unwanted affection of an older woman.'

The icy-breasted Spanish prince sailed from Corunna in July 1554, together with a fleet of 100 ships and several thousand troops, horses and mules bound for the Low Countries. Among his entourage of nobles were the Duke of Alba, High Steward to Charles V, the Count of Egmont, who had helped draw up the marriage contract in London, and Philip's most trusted adviser and confidant, the Count of Feria. The party disembarked at Southampton on 20th July, Philip met the Queen for the first time three days later in Winchester, and they were married in that city's cathedral on the 25th, the Feast of St James, Spain's patron saint.

Philip's introduction to England was not the happiest: Hampshire was experiencing three days of heavy and persistent rain. When he rode to Mass in Southampton, he had to borrow an Englishman's cape and hat, and when he left to ride to Winchester two days later, his red felt cloak, white satin trunks and doublet were soaked and spattered with mud. He was obliged to stop at a monastery outside the city in order to change his clothes before his meeting with Mary in the bishop's palace that evening. Before the wedding service the following morning, a message from Brussels declared that Philip had been proclaimed king of Naples, raising him from princely status to something like equality with the queen of England. The announcement was made by Feria, waving a document signed by the Emperor, as Philip entered the cathedral. Marriage to Mary now confirmed Philip as king of England and Ireland, but he would never be crowned. He was king consort without any power of state.

After the wedding, for which, we are told, Mary wore a dress of white damask embroidered with gold and pearls, a black headdress and on her breast a large ruby, the celebrations included dancing, at which Philip did not distinguish himself. However, it is reasonable to assume that some of the Spanish nobles would have danced with some of the Queen's ladies-in-waiting, attempting a conversation probably limited by their ignorance of the other's language. If not on that day, then soon afterwards, the Count of Feria noticed and became attracted to Jane Dormer. His affection for her, according to Henry Clifford, 'as much grounded upon her virtuous parts as on the rareness of her beauty... considering all the parts of this fair lady, esteemed him happy who should enjoy her'. A poet of the time, Richard Edwards, wrote of Jane that she was 'a darline and of shuche lively hewe that who so fedes his eyes on her may sone her bewte vue'. However, the physical appearance of Mary's other ladies did not impress the Spanish courtiers, who judged them to be unsuitably dressed and 'indelicate when they are seated'. The members of Philip's entourage were no doubt frustrated by the absence of their wives and ladies, who had not been invited to accompany the royal party to England.

Although her half-Spanish mistress had just married a Spaniard, and there had been previous 'political' royal marriages such as John of Gaunt's to the daughter of Pedro the Cruel, Anglo-Spanish personal relationships among the upper classes of their countries were not common in the 16th century. Apart from Edward Courtenay, who was directing his affections at both Mary and her lady-in-waiting, Jane's suitors included several members of the Howard family. There was Thomas Howard, who had just inherited the dukedom of Norfolk; his brother Henry, subsequently Earl of Northampton, who in spite of his closet Catholicism and support for Mary Queen of Scots, kept his head throughout Elizabeth's reign; and his cousin Charles, Lord Howard of Effingham, later raised to the earldom of Nottingham, Elizabeth's Lord High Admiral and commander of the English forces against the Spanish Armada; but she turned them all down.

These three men were her contemporaries, all of them teenagers in 1554, while Feria was more than twice Jane's age. In the atmosphere at court, with her beloved mistress married to a Spanish prince, it was not so surprising that Jane should become enamoured of a Spanish nobleman who was Philip's closest confidant and adviser. But it was not popular with her father and stepmother, nor with her Sidney uncles, who thought that a nice young and well-connected Englishman would be much more suitable.

II

Jane marries her *novio*

THE TITLE OF Feria is taken from a small town in Extremadura, south-west Spain, which, together with Zafra and the pueblo of La Parra, were granted to the then head of the Suarez de Figueroa dynasty by the young king of Castile, Enrique III, in 1394. The family had aristocratic origins in Galicia, with connections to the Order of Santiago, and the Figueroa coat of arms—five green fig leaves on a field of gold—was won while Galicia was under Moorish authority. (The story went that 100 maidens were rescued from the Moors' clutches by the noble Figueroas fighting for their virtue in a grove of fig trees.) After the Reconquest the Figueroas moved south, taking control of large tracts of land in Extremadura and, through marriage, in Andalusia as well. From the early 15th century the family, now the most important dynasty in south-west Spain, gave their patronage to several religious orders, also to the arts and especially to Extremaduran poets and to a Renaissance playwright, Diego Sanchez de Badajoz. The 1st Count of Feria was created in 1460; Philip's man was the 5th, born in 1523 and inheriting the title on the death of his elder brother Pedro in 1552. Feria had four brothers, one of whom became Bishop of Sigüenza, and one sister. He had served in several military campaigns in the army of Charles V and joined Prince Philip's court in Valladolid in 1548, aged 25, where he held the position of Captain of the Spanish Guard. In 1554 Sanchez de Badajoz's nephew, who was chaplain to the Count, dedicated his uncle's posthumous work, *Recopilacion en metro*, to Feria, who paid for its publication while he was in England.

Feria has been described as 'not particularly gifted, but he was loyal, personable and without ambition. He was also transparently honest, and this seems to have been the quality that Philip most admired in him.' Sir

Gomez Suárez de Figueroa y Córdoba, 5th Count and 1st Duke of Feria.

John Mason, ambassador at the Emperor's court in Brussels, meeting him on his way to England in 1554, reported to Mary that he was 'a right wise and grave counsellor'. Perhaps the ambassador did not have time to discover that Feria could also be stubborn, prickly, outspoken and unwilling to compromise—not ideal qualities for his future role as a diplomat. The historian JE Neale described him as 'a typical grandee of Spain, devoid of humour, proud and patronising'. He was also a strict Catholic, having recently become a member of the Society of Jesus, founded by Ignatius of Loyola in 1540. Pedro de Ribadeneyra, a follower of Loyola and friend of Feria, wrote that he represented his monarch with 'great authority, courage and prudence', though many would have taken issue with the third quality. When he arrived in England in 1554, Feria was, in Jean Plaidy's account in her novel, *The Spanish Bridegroom*, engaged to a Spanish lady of noble birth (in fact his brother Pedro's daughter Catalina, Marchioness of Priego, the title inherited from Feria's mother). But his developing relationship with Jane soon had Philip's blessing, and the Spanish fiancée stayed in Spain. (She married instead one of Feria's younger brothers.)

Feria remained in England with Philip as his trusted adviser until September 1555, when they both left for Flanders. Charles V was beginning the process of his abdication, handing over the Netherlands to his son in October and the Spanish crown in January 1556. Philip did return as king of Spain to England the following year, but stayed only four months before leaving England and his queen for the last time. Feria accompanied Philip to England on this second occasion and was appointed his ambassador in London in December 1557. The relationship with Jane matured during this time, and Feria proposed 'after satisfying himself that her pedigree was in order'. Mary gave her consent for them to marry, but asked them to wait until Philip was back in London and the royal couple could together attend the wedding. In the event Jane and Feria were married six weeks after Mary died.

Jane was not just one of several ladies-in-waiting to the Queen. She was so close a confidante that, Henry Clifford tells us, 'she slept in her bedchamber, many times with her; she read together with her Our Lady's office….At table, [Mary] eat the meat that the hand of Jane Dormer carved for her.' In spite of the reputation she would acquire as 'Bloody Mary', the Queen made many visits to the poor, often with Jane accompanying her. She would give alms to the children and listen to complaints, instructing Jane to take a note of them. Jane was at this time still a teenager (aged 17 in 1555), and her mistress, who was 22 years older, looked upon her in some ways as a daughter and always kept a maternal eye on her. At the same time, while Mary was surrounded by enemies and dogged by ill health during her unhappy and difficult reign, the youthful Jane was able to give her, according to one commentator, 'the peace and loyalty she needed'. Mary remarked that Jane deserved a very good husband and that she knew not the man worthy of her.

There was another lady of greater significance at court, about eight years older than the Queen, who had been in her service since before Jane was born. Susan White, born of Essex landowning parents, came into contact with Mary and entered her service shortly before Henry VIII married Anne Boleyn and had his marriage to Mary's mother Catherine annulled. Mary was declared illegitimate, her servants were dismissed and she lost her rights to the succession. Three years later she reluctantly agreed to submit to Henry's authority ('most humbly prostrate'), after the death of her mother and the execution of Anne Boleyn. Her household was reinstated and Susan, now the widow of Thomas Tonge, rejoined her, with the approval of Thomas Cromwell. Tonge had been a herald for some 20 years before he was appointed Clarence herald in 1534 and married Susan, but held the position for less than two years before he died in March 1536. Susan clearly enjoyed the title and was known as Mistress Clarencius, or Clarencieux, for the rest of her life.

Having served as principal lady in Princess Mary's household, Susan was appointed Mistress of the Robes and chief lady of the Queen's Privy Chamber when Mary became queen. These positions seem to have included shopping for the Queen, giving advice on her dress, arranging to pay her gambling debts (Mary enjoyed playing cards and 'pass-dice') and at least some of the duties performed for kings by the Groom of the Stool. Most importantly, the relationship between mistress and servant was so close and trusting that Mary consulted her on the question of marriage to Philip, which Susan encouraged. When the imperial envoy Simon Renard began to broach the matter with the Queen, he soon realised that it was important that Susan be included in discussions taking place with the Spanish royal representatives. She was said to have had several meetings at a private house in London with Diego de Mendoza, one of Philip's envoys. When Mary formally accepted Philip's proposal, she swore an oath of acceptance in a ceremony attended only by Renard and Susan, following which Renard deemed it worth reporting to the Emperor that Susan supported 'our cause to the utmost'. She was rewarded with gifts from Philip when he came to England to marry the Queen in 1554, and over the next couple of years Mary gave her a manor and an advowson in Essex together with several grants of land in the county.

She also acquired other possessions, and not always by the most honourable means. When the Venetian ambassador, Giovanni Michieli, made his report at the end of his mission in 1557, he disclosed that the Queen's *cameria principale*, 'Mistress Clarentia', had persuaded him that Mary needed a coach and horses and that it was his duty to make her a gift before he returned to Venice. When the Queen was presented with the coach—she had no need of another one—she passed it on to her Mistress of the Robes, who was delighted that her ruse had been successful.

Three months after the wedding, Mary announced that she was pregnant. The following spring she moved to Hampton Court for the 'lying-in', and she lay there until the beginning of August, when she finally had to accept that there was no baby. Philip had been longing to go back to the Low Countries, but he was persuaded by Simon Renard that he should not leave until England's return to Catholic Christendom had gained general acceptance in the country. Otherwise, Renard said somewhat melodramatically, 'religion will be overthrown, the Queen's person will be in danger and Parliament will not meet'. Philip left his wife on 29th August 1555: it would be more than 18 months before he came back to her, and 14 weeks later he was gone for good. During this brief period he persuaded Mary—against the terms of their marriage treaty—to give support to his war on France, which resulted, in January 1558, in the loss of Calais, England's sole remaining possession in France. The responsibility was not entirely Philip's, and he was reluctant to accept Feria's statement—on what evidence, one wonders—that, after Calais had fallen, the number of Englishmen attending Mass fell by two-thirds. This was the final misery of Mary's reign, prompting her famous lament to Susan Clarencius not long before she died: 'When I am dead and opened, you shall find Calais lying in my heart.'

Having reluctantly agreed that the monastery lands confiscated by her father should not be returned to the church, Mary and Philip had persuaded Parliament in November 1554 that the church should be returned to papal jurisdiction; all anti-papal laws were repealed and the Heresy Acts were revived. Less than a month later, in February 1555, the burnings began. Cardinal Reginald Pole, the Pope's Legate, was now back in England and, together with several of her bishops, encouraged the Queen to deal with heretics with the utmost severity. She may have needed little urging, but by the summer of 1555 she was inclined to believe that her false pregnancy was God's punishment for her tolerance of Protestants in the early part of her reign. Archbishop Cranmer was forced to watch Bishops Latimer and Ridley being burnt at the stake, and when he duly went into the flames in March 1556, Pole replaced him as the last Catholic Archbishop of Canterbury. The number of burnings between 1555 and Mary's death in 1558 has been put at 283.

It is not to excuse the Marian persecutions to point out that Mary had to struggle throughout her life with paternal ill treatment, with ill health and without the affection of her people or the husband whom she genuinely loved. As a child she was betrothed to a French king (Francis I), a future French king (Henry, Duke of Orleans), a Holy Roman Emperor (Charles V) and a brother of the king of Portugal, then was denied the title of princess when her father married Anne Boleyn. She was declared a bastard, forced to act as lady-in-waiting to her half-sister Elizabeth, and never saw her mother during the last four years of Catherine's life.

This took its toll on Mary's health, both mental and physical, and for the rest of her life she suffered from abdominal pains and other ailments every year during autumn and winter. Her first phantom pregnancy was probably attributable to amenorrhea, and at the beginning of 1558 her 'pregnant' condition was thought to be dropsy which, together with the onset of uterine cancer, ended her life in November of that year.

Having fled to East Anglia when Edward VI died, and then returned as queen after Northumberland surrendered, Mary showed great courage in facing down Wyatt's rebellion six months later. She was never popular once she had decided to marry a Spanish prince, though her people might have looked on her with less hostility had she followed the advice of her husband and the imperial ambassador, Simon Renard, who counselled against her extreme measures in burning Protestants at the stake. While they had no moral objection to an English inquisition, they feared that it would exacerbate anti-Catholic and, more relevantly, anti-Spanish feelings. Renard warned of a popular revolt, and Philip took the uncharacteristically moderate view, not shared by his wife, that the English would be more successfully brought back to the true faith by education and persuasion rather than by the methods against heretics employed in his own country. Though determined to get rid of heretics with extreme cruelty, Mary was better disposed towards her relatives and those nobles who had conspired against her. She was reluctant to order Lady Jane Grey's execution, she spared a number of those who had plotted with Northumberland to deny her the throne and, against Renard's advice, she refused to have her half-sister Elizabeth beheaded when she was suspected of complicity in Wyatt's rebellion.

Queen Mary's reign ended without a Catholic heir, without her husband at her side and with ten people burnt to death in the last two weeks of her life. Her last years were marked also by another plot to overthrow her, this time with the support of France, and by poor harvests, floods and famine to make her people's lives more miserable. Once all hopes of pregnancy had passed, she was having to accept that her half-sister would succeed her, though she tried to convince herself that Elizabeth looked like a young musician, Mark Smeaton. He was said to have been one of Anne Boleyn's supposed lovers, whom she kept in her 'sweetmeat cupboard' to await her pleasure. At least Mary was comforted, as she lay dying, by 'good dreams… seeing many little children like angels play before her, singing pleasing notes, giving her more than earthly comfort'.

Jane Dormer and Mary's other ladies may have been unhappy to learn of the burnings of Protestant martyrs which were taking place a few miles away in Smithfield, in Essex, Kent and elsewhere in the south of England, but their loyalty to the Queen was unconditional. As a devout Catholic, and in conversation with the Count of Feria, Jane would have been aware of the practices of the Inquisition in Spain, and Feria may have told her of his unsuccessful attempts to introduce the Jesuit Order into England. Most important to her, however, was the health of her mistress and, from 1557, the prospect of marriage to Feria and the threat of a Protestant England under Elizabeth. Having returned to Brussels with his master Philip in July 1557, Feria went with him to Cambrai in August and on to St Quentin to witness the battle of that name against the French. Before the end of that year Feria was back in England, this time as ambassador. It was during the next six months that his relationship with Jane grew more intimate and, with Mary's approval, marriage was contemplated. Neither of them was fluent in the other's language, but Jane, almost uniquely among young Englishwomen of her age and class, was able to speak some Spanish. She had the half-Spanish Queen Mary as her tutor, and her maternal grandfather Sir William Sidney may have passed on his knowledge of the language from the time he had spent in Spain at the beginning of Henry VIII's reign.

Feria's main preoccupations on Philip's behalf were with the recovery of Calais for England after its loss in January 1558 (the town was taken by the Duke of Guise, Mary Queen of Scots' uncle); the question of breaking off relations with Scotland (Philip refused to declare war on the country); and trade between England and the Hanseatic towns. At the same time he was reporting on the Queen's health and the expected succession of Elizabeth. In March Feria told Philip that 'it seems to me that [the Queen] is making herself believe that she is with child, although she does not own up to it'. But nobody else believed it, and her health began to suffer. At the beginning of May Feria was reporting to Philip that the Queen 'is somewhat better than she was a few days ago, but she sleeps badly, is weak and suffers from melancholy; and her indisposition results in business being handled more slowly than need be'. The following month, instructed by Philip and without the Queen's knowledge, Feria went to see Elizabeth at Ashridge, to discuss the succession and a proposal from the king of Sweden that his son should marry her. He did not report the details of this meeting until he was recalled by Philip to Brussels in July.

Feria spent less than four months in Flanders, then was sent back to London from Arras at the beginning of November. Philip wrote to the Privy Council, to the Queen's physicians and to Cardinal Pole, saying that Feria would 'serve the Queen during her illness, being unable to proceed to England in person as I would have wished to do'. Philip was also being kept informed of his wife's health by his envoy Christophe d'Assonleville, a member of the King's Flemish Council, whom he had sent to London and reported in October that the Queen was 'better at present than she has been since she fell ill'. But Philip, knowing that her days were numbered, was more concerned with peace negotiations with France, which had begun in mid-October, and anxious to get back to Spain following the death of his father, Charles V, at the monastery of Yuste in western Spain on 21st September. (The news did not reach Philip in northern France for another five weeks.)

Feria arrived in England on 9th November, in company with a Portuguese physician, and went to St James's Palace that evening to deliver a letter from Philip to Mary, but she was barely conscious and unable to read it. Having already met her Privy Council earlier in the day, it was clear to Feria that Mary's life was coming to an end and that Philip would no longer carry the title of king of England. Feria learnt that Mary had finally accepted, in the last week of October, that Elizabeth would succeed her on the throne. In a codicil to her will she had not named her half-sister but had written that the crown should pass to 'the next heir in law'. The following day, 'at the private house of a knight, 13 miles from London' (Brocket Hall in Hertfordshire), Feria was received by the still Princess Elizabeth. Their lengthy conversation was conducted mostly in private and probably in Italian. In Philippa Gregory's novel, *The Queen's Fool*, Feria dines with Elizabeth, seated on her right with Robert Dudley opposite him. Jane, who brings messages from the Queen, is told that 'the man you love, Count Feria, the Spanish ambassador, who once demanded [Elizabeth's] death... now brings love letters from the Queen's own husband. Betrayal is no new thing in England. If you won't break bread with men with false hearts you will starve to death, Jane.' But she refuses to sit at Elizabeth's table, and tells her after dinner that Mary will name her as her heir if Elizabeth will swear to keep the country in the true faith. She raises her hand and swears.

When Jane returned to London she had a slight fever, and Mary sent her to the royal physician. On her return Jane insisted to Mary that she was quite well, to which Mary apparently replied: 'So am not I.' D'Assonleville wrote to Philip on the 8th that 'fears about the outcome of the Queen's illness are increasing from day to day'. Feria wrote on the 14th, but his letter did not reach Philip in Brussels until after Mary's death at dawn on the 17th aged 42, having spent most of her last days in prayer, and accepting the host as a 'sacred medicine'. Jane was one of Mary's ladies who helped Susan Clarencius to lay out the Queen's body. Later that day they learnt that Cardinal Pole had died.

In his long letter Feria told his master that extreme unction had been administered to his wife and that 'there is no hope of her life... each hour I think they will come to inform me of her death, so rapidly does her condition deteriorate from one day to the next'. He had briefed the council on Philip's dealings with France as well as on Mary's imminent demise, reporting that 'these councillors are extremely frightened of what Madam Elizabeth will do with them. They have received me well, but somewhat as they would a man who came with bulls from a dead pope.'

Much of the letter, however, was concerned with Elizabeth and her future relations with Philip. Philip's letter to Elizabeth, which Feria gave her at Brocket Hall, expressed his hopes for continuing good relations between Spain and England, for peace negotiations with France, and for her marriage, possibly to the Duke of Savoy. As a mark of friendship, Philip wrote the letter in his own hand. When Feria had dined with Elizabeth on the 10th she told him she was grateful that Philip had helped to secure her release from house arrest in 1554. She had been detained by Mary in the Tower for her suspected part in Wyatt's rebellion. According to Jane, Philip 'delivered [Elizabeth] not only from extreme punishment but procured her liberty to return to the Court' when he came to England. Mary had in fact already released her half-sister from the Tower two months before Philip's arrival, but she remained under house arrest for the rest of that year. As Elizabeth travelled from the Tower to her continuing custody at Woodstock in May 1554, she spent one night on the way as the guest of Jane's father, Sir William Dormer, at West Wycombe—when she may have enquired how his daughter was getting on with the Queen. The following year Elizabeth went from Woodstock to Hatfield, when she may also have spent a night at the invitation of Sir William, this time at Ascott, where the Dormers kept a resident priest who, it was said, never emerged from his chamber.

At their meeting Feria tried to remind Elizabeth that it was Philip who had persuaded Mary to recognise her as her successor. But Elizabeth refused to acknowledge this, saying that it was the people who had decided she should be queen. (It was in fact her father who, by the Act of Succession of 1544, and his last will in 1546, determined that, if Mary died without a legitimate heir, Elizabeth should succeed her.) Elizabeth thought Feria's attitude was 'very superior, like a true Spaniard'. Feria wrote to Philip of Elizabeth: *'Ella es una mujer vanissima y aguda'*—'She is a very vain and clever woman... She must have been thoroughly schooled in the manner in which her father conducted his affairs... I am very much afraid that she will not be well-disposed in matters of religion, for I see her inclined to govern through men who are believed to be heretics and I am told that all the women around her definitely are.' In her subsequent meetings and communications with him over the next six months, Feria was frequently exasperated, not only by her 'heresy' but by her refusal to decide on a husband; and she usually got the better of him.

Feria was rather put out when Elizabeth told him that Mary had lost the affection of her people by marrying a foreigner. He replied, unconvincingly, that Philip had been well loved, but accepted that the English did not usually like foreigners. However, he said, '*a mi ya me tenían por Ingles*': 'they already thought of me as an Englishman'—a statement which, in view of the low opinion he held and expressed of most of Mary's and Elizabeth's ministers, was unlikely to apply to anyone, except perhaps the young woman whom he hoped to marry. Instructed by Mary, Jane had already handed over the royal jewels to Elizabeth at Hatfield. Once the new queen had succeeded her, Jane was charged by Feria with giving Elizabeth two rings which Mary had given Philip, also jewels which Philip and Charles V had presented to Mary as wedding gifts. Some confusion over the inventory of the crown jewels led to suspicion, on the part of Elizabeth's ladies-in-waiting, that Jane had lost, or held on to, some items, but she was soon exonerated.

The accession of Elizabeth gave Feria the opportunity to rail against various ministers in most undiplomatic terms. Writing to Philip on 21st November, he called Mary's Lord Chamberlain, Lord Hastings, '*ruin*' ('contemptible'), declaring that 'really this country is more fit to be dealt with sword in hand than by cajolery, for there are neither funds, nor soldiers, nor heads, nor forces, and yet it is overflowing with every other necessary of life'. In the three days since Mary's death 'things are in such a hurly-burly and confusion that fathers do not know their own children... That accursed Cardinal [Pole] left 12 bishoprics to be filled, which will now be given to as many ministers of Lucifer.' He had no time for the Queen's Councillors—earlier that year he had written to Philip that 'I am at my wits' end, God knows, what to do with these people'—yet fancifully imagined that they thought of him as an Englishman, as one of them. The eminent 19th-century historian, Martin Hume, who edited the Spanish Calendar of State Papers, was of the opinion that Feria 'hated England and Englishmen with a fierce intensity' and had no understanding of the country or its people. His feelings may not have been quite so extreme, but they did not immediately qualify him as an ideal ambassador to the English court. For the rest of his tenure, he did what he could to encourage resistance to Elizabeth among English Catholics.

The question of Elizabeth's marriage occupied Feria during the months before and after Mary's death. Among the prospective husbands put forward for her were Prince Eric of Sweden; Duke Adolphus, the king of

Denmark's brother; the Holy Roman Emperor's son, Archduke Ferdinand; his youngest son Archduke Charles; the Duke of Savoy; and Philip himself. However, this was largely a waste of time, since Elizabeth had made it clear that she would not repeat Mary's mistake in marrying a foreigner.

By the end of 1558 Feria had to acknowledge that Elizabeth had lost any respect which she may have had for him before she became queen. The feeling was mutual and he asked Philip to replace him as ambassador. As soon as Elizabeth ascended the throne, Feria realised that he needed someone at his side with better negotiating skills and more diplomatic cunning than he possessed. He was too intolerant, too transparent, too impetuous and lacked the suppleness and guile needed to deal with Elizabeth and Cecil. In early December 1558, at Feria's request, Alvaro de la Quadra, bishop of Aquila, arrived in London to assist him. A Neapolitan of Spanish extraction, he was both patient and unscrupulous, described by a fellow bishop as 'a clever and crafty old fox', who took Feria's place in May 1559 and remained as resident ambassador until his death four years later.

In a letter from Philip to Elizabeth soon after Mary died—in which he expressed his 'confidence that she will find in me all the promptitude of goodwill and affection that she can desire'—he also gave Feria a glowing reference. But his ambassador's relationship with Elizabeth was never going to approach the understanding which he had enjoyed with her predecessor, and it was not long before he was obliged to move out of his apartment in the palace. However, in the first weeks of Elizabeth's reign, he had more than Anglo-Spanish political relations on his mind. He was intent on making an Anglo-Spanish match with Jane Dormer, despite opposition from both their families. According to the gossiping Venetian ambassador, Feria, who was frequently in debt, was due to receive at least 40,000 crowns as a dowry when he married his niece, but he was now 'in a transport of love' for Jane. When Mary died Jane was not invited to serve the new queen—she might have been, had Feria gone back to Spain—and went to stay with her grandmother Lady Dormer at the Savoy palace. Two weeks after Mary's funeral, Jane and Feria, concerned that they might not be able to marry according to the rites of the Catholic church, and that Elizabeth would not give her approval, were married secretly in the Savoy chapel on 29th December, the Feast of St Thomas of Canterbury. It was the only union between a Spanish and an English courtier to result from Philip's time in England.* He was aged 38 and she was a week away from her 21st birthday. Feria took his bride to Durham House, the Spanish ambassador's residence a little further along the Strand from the Savoy chapel, where they lived for the next few months. Catherine of Aragon had lived at Durham House after the death of her first husband, Arthur; and Lady Jane Grey and Guildford Dudley were married there. Mary restored the house when she came to the throne and made it available to the Spanish ambassador. It became the residence of Jane's uncle, Sir Henry Sidney, after 1565. (Today there is a modern building called Durham House, in the street of that name, but without the view of the river which the occupants enjoyed in the 16th century.)

Feria presumably had Philip's approval for the marriage, but in a long letter which carries the date of his wedding, 29th December, he makes no mention of it. While it was surely a happy day for him, he was expressing to Philip his unhappiness at the way he was being treated by Elizabeth. In a tone which verges on the chippy and self-pitying, Feria wrote:

'I am afraid that one fine day we shall find this woman married, and I shall be the last man in the place to know anything about it. And yet, while I do not know of a single thing that is going on, I hear the Queen said a few days ago that I was too well informed about English affairs to be allowed to stay here, and that like a true Spaniard I was very proud, and that she would be glad if your Majesty would recall me and send someone else... I try to overlook many things and not to seem to take offence at anything or to appear inquisitive, but their enmity and evil consciences make them so cautious and suspicious that they think I know everything, and in return for all my wishes to please them I believe they would like to see me thrown into the river, that is to say, she and her adherents.'

Clearly Feria knew that, in a country that was forsaking the true religion, and under a queen who had taken against him and was refusing to give him rooms in the palace which he had previously enjoyed, his and Jane's time would soon be up. Relations with the Queen were not improved when, in spite of several invitations, Feria declined to attend her coronation on 15th January. One of the few Englishmen whom Feria respected was John

---

* Jane's cousin, Margaret Harrington, had no position at court but she married a
  Spanish courtier whom she had met in England during Mary's reign.

Boxall, archdeacon of Ely and Mary's Secretary of State. Through Feria he tried unsuccessfully to persuade Elizabeth to reject the new prayer book, and the following year he was imprisoned for refusing to take the oath of supremacy. (The Act of Supremacy was passed in 1559.)

Another man whom Feria thought he could do business with was Sir Thomas Parry, the Queen's Comptroller of the Household. During the winter of 1559 Feria had conversations with Parry about religion and the Queen's duty and he continued to convince himself that he could arrange a marriage between Philip and Elizabeth, even that she wanted the marriage but that the Council was doing its best to dissuade her. Feria had several meetings with the Queen but he was fast losing patience with her. With his customary bluntness, he wrote to his master: 'She seems to me incomparably more feared than her sister, and gives her orders and has her way as absolutely as her father did... It is very troublesome to negotiate with this woman, as she is naturally changeable, and those who surround her are so blind and bestial that they do not at all understand the state of affairs.' In particular his irritation was directed at Sir William Cecil and Sir Nicholas Throckmorton,* both of whom he called knaves.

Philip wrote to Feria to ask him to propose his marriage to Elizabeth, saying how important such a match would be 'to Christianity and the preservation of religion' and arrogantly, or naively, assuming she would accept his terms: that she apply to the Pope for absolution and embrace the Catholic faith—which she had never done during Mary's reign. Having asked Elizabeth to convert, Philip stated with all seriousness, as if her agreement were a foregone conclusion, that 'it will be evident and manifest that I am serving the Lord in marrying her and that she has been converted by my act'. His more practical concern was to keep France at bay, and in particular the Dauphin's wife Mary, who was also Queen of Scots with a claim to the English throne. However, Philip and Feria were both displaying extraordinary arrogance and ignorance. Philip may have convinced himself, with Feria's encouragement, that he was rendering a service to God and to Spain by marrying Elizabeth. And Feria had told his master, immediately after Mary's death, that if Elizabeth were to decide to marry a foreigner, 'she will at once fix her eyes on your Majesty'. This may have been

---

* Throckmorton was appointed ambassador to France in May 1559.

no more than complaisant flattery, but his confidence did not last long, as he came to realise that he was dealing with someone much smarter than he had anticipated. Did neither the King nor Feria have any understanding of the English people? Having disliked the idea of a Spanish marriage in 1554, and blamed Philip for the loss of Calais, how much more opposed to Philip would they be now, after the tragic experience of Mary's reign? Having married an Englishwoman and spent time in England, Feria liked to think that he knew the English. But he seemed incapable of recognising that the people as a whole wanted independence from Spain and the papacy. Although Jane had spent her formative years in the service of a half-Spanish Catholic queen, and would later be associated with English Jesuits in exile bent on getting rid of the 'bastard' Protestant queen, she never shared her husband's irredeemably hostile view of Elizabeth as 'a daughter of the Devil'.

Elizabeth strung Feria and Philip along for a while. A peace treaty with France was being negotiated, and she would be in a stronger bargaining position with Philip as her suitor. Continuing her strategy of bluff with Feria, Elizabeth told him that she must consult Parliament but that if she decided to marry at all she would choose Philip. Now he was not so sure the marriage was a good idea: he had been absent from England for most of Mary's reign and would have to be out of England again for much of the time due to the claims of his other dominions. Admitting, at least to himself, that he had hardly been a popular king of England, he told Feria it was 'necessary for me to take counsel and maturely consider it in all its bearings before I send you my decision'. One of his concerns was the expenses he would incur in England and the inability of his treasury to meet them. The King was not to be hurried; he continued to procrastinate, prompting Feria to tell Quadra: 'It is only with great trouble that he can be persuaded to decide anything.'

A few weeks later Elizabeth told Feria that she could not marry Philip because she was a heretic, and anyway she would not dream of marrying her brother-in-law. One might have thought that both Feria and Philip could have worked that out as soon as Mary died, but Elizabeth had few equals in the art of dissembling and prevarication, before acting as she had originally intended. By the spring of 1559, accepting that he was going to get nowhere with Elizabeth, Philip turned to an alliance with France and another Elizabeth, princess of Valois and daughter of Henri II, who became his third wife as part of the peace settlement. (They were married by proxy in Paris in June.) Queen Elizabeth is said to have chided Feria that the King could not have been much in love with her, as he did not have the patience to wait four months. When Feria responded that it was she who had turned Philip down, Elizabeth said that she had never given him a definite answer. Philip assured Elizabeth that his marriage alliance would not affect their friendly relations, while in meetings with Feria she continued to get the better of the hapless ambassador. He did think he had scored a few points when, at his urging, she agreed not to call herself 'Head of the Church', but then decided she would take the title of 'Governess of the Church' instead.

Philip and Feria now resolved that Elizabeth should be persuaded to take Philip's cousin, the Holy Roman Emperor's son Archduke Ferdinand, as her husband, but the same religious objections would apply, and anyway Elizabeth made it clear she would not agree to marry anyone she had not set eyes on. (Ferdinand was in fact already secretly married to a woman not of royal blood.) The rumour was being put about that the Queen could not have children; but the more persistent rumour was that she was enamoured of Robert Dudley and would marry him as soon as his wife, who was suffering from breast cancer, did the decent thing and died. Feria picked up the gossip and noted that 'it is even said that her Majesty visits him in his chamber day and night'.

At about this time Feria was sent to France, at the insistence of Henri II, as a diplomatic hostage for the peace treaty between Spain, France and England which was signed at Cateau-Cambresis on 3rd April. It was said, however, that this was a French ruse to get Feria out of the Queen's way and stop his continuing attempts to press her into a Habsburg marriage. Later that year one of Elizabeth's close confidantes, Mary Sidney, married to Jane's uncle, Sir Henry Sidney, was trying to convince Quadra that the Queen wished to marry the Emperor's 19-year-old son Archduke Charles. But since Lady Sidney was Robert Dudley's sister, her motives may have been suspect.

Exasperated both by the Queen's volatile nature and by his master's indecision, Feria began to hatch a bizarre plan while he was in France. Under

Henry VIII's will, his sister Mary Tudor's granddaughter, Katherine Grey, sister of Jane Grey, was next in line of succession if Elizabeth should die childless. Feria was afraid that, if Elizabeth were to marry Dudley, Henri would take advantage of the civil disorder which might follow by attempting to install his daughter-in-law Mary Queen of Scots on the English throne. Feria's idea was that Katherine should be ready to pre-empt any such French plot, possibly by being smuggled out of England to Spain to await events. Katherine had apparently convinced Feria that she was a Catholic, and she was happy to communicate with Jane, whom she had known when they were both members of Mary's court. Whatever Jane may have thought of her husband's scheming, she was not going to be a co-conspirator with him, preferring to exert her calming influence when he returned from the signing of the peace treaty in France. Jane now knew she was pregnant and was happy to spend time at Durham House with her embroidery and in the company of Susan Clarencius, who joined her household after Mary's death. The impulsive Feria had had enough of London, and asked Philip to let him come back to Flanders, where he thought he could have a more positive influence on his master. Philip consented and Quadra was appointed ambassador in Feria's place, as he prepared to leave England for the last time. The Katherine stratagem was not going anywhere: Henri died after a jousting accident, Mary became queen of France, and the following year Katherine married Lord Hertford, of the Seymour family, without Elizabeth's permission and was imprisoned in the Tower. Katherine quickly went out of the Ferias' life while, less than year later, Mary Queen of Scots and France would become Jane's new best friend.

When Feria came to take his leave of the Queen, in the last week of May, he was said to be disappointed not to receive a parting gift from her. More importantly, with her permission Feria arranged for a number of Catholics, possibly as many as 100, to travel to Flanders at the same time. Among them were 12 Carthusian monks and three lay brothers, accompanied by their prior, Maurice Chauncy; nuns from the convents of Syon, Brentford and Dartford Priory; and various priests and former courtiers known to Philip's entourage during Mary's reign. Some of Elizabeth's councillors tried to dissuade her from allowing such an exodus, but she would not revoke her permission and they all took ship for Flanders, under Philip's protection and with their passage paid by Feria. Some would remain there, in Louvain and Mechlin, while a few travelled on to Spain. Contact with the Ferias would not be lost, and over the next few years a network of exiled English Catholics would be established, with Jane, Countess of Feria at its centre.

III

A new life in Flanders

ONCE THE Count of Feria had left for Flanders, Durham House became the residence of his replacement as ambassador, Alvaro de la Quadra, Bishop of Aquila. However, Feria had stipulated that the Countess should remain in the house until her departure for Flanders two months later. During these summer weeks of 1559 a number of visitors, relations and friends of Jane, came to see her at the embassy in the hope of travelling with her, away from the Protestant England which Elizabeth was fast establishing. The Act of Uniformity had just been passed, prescribing the use of the Book of Common Prayer and requiring all people to go to church once a week or pay a fine of 12 pence. However, Catholic manoeuvres were active in pursuit of a husband for Elizabeth, and the Emperor's envoy, Count von Helfenstein, on his mission to arrange an archducal marriage, was put up at Durham House when he came to London.

Philip authorised Feria to arrange for a member of the royal household to escort Jane to Flanders. Don Juan de Ayala had been with Feria in London the previous year, and was now sent back to England to prepare for Jane's departure. Thinking that Elizabeth was delaying her permission for Jane to leave the country, Feria wrote to Quadra from Ghent, saying he wanted his wife to leave as soon as possible and without seeing the Queen. But she had had royal permission to take a number of friends, relations and attendants with her and thought it right to say a formal goodbye at Eltham Palace, Greenwich, where Elizabeth was staying. Jane left Durham House on 24th July in the company of Quadra and Ayala, but her audience with Elizabeth did not go smoothly. According to Cecil's account, she arrived at court at one o'clock in the afternoon, on her way to the Kent coast. She was now seven months pregnant and was apparently kept waiting by the

Queen for what Quadra considered was an unreasonable time before the start of her journey. She refused to sit down while she waited, not wishing to be disrespectful to the Queen. In spite of the good relations which Quadra had established with Elizabeth, by showing her more patience and understanding than had Feria, he now began shouting angrily at the Lord Chamberlain that the Countess could wait no longer and that her husband was not the Queen's vassal. When Jane was ushered into the Queen's privy chamber, leaving Quadra outside, the two women, according to Cecil, 'had very much familiar and loving talk', Jane apologised for the ambassador's behaviour and she 'departed with very good contentation'. 'Surely the Bishop [Quadra] forgat himself very much,' Cecil wrote; 'all he can pretend is that the Countess is with child, and had to ride to Rochester 12 or 13 miles off,* both of which were well considered by the Queen, so that she was dismissed about three of the clock, so as to have six hours before night to ride her journey; and considering the heat of the day more meeter to be ridden toward the evening than nigh the midday.' This letter was written to Sir Thomas Chaloner, who had just been appointed ambassador to the Spanish court in Ghent.

Feria was displeased, referring to 'a great misliking of his wife's evil usage at the Queen's hands', though he would only have heard Quadra's version of the incident. Cecil described Quadra's behaviour as 'uncourtly', and his speech as 'disordered', which was probably Jane's view too, though she may not have said so to her husband. At all events, Jane and Elizabeth parted on amicable terms; they were not close, but Elizabeth respected Jane's childhood friendship with Edward and her long and trusting relationship with Mary. Elizabeth and Jane continued to communicate at a distance from time to time over the next decade, despite her husband's persistent hostility to the Queen and her own scheming on Philip's behalf in the Catholic cause.

Before Jane was able to leave Elizabethan England (she was never to return to the country of her birth), she needed a passport granting permission not only to her but to various attendants—six gentlewomen, a laundress, a yeoman of the wardrobe, five gentlemen, two pages, two chaplains, seven gentlemen's men—to take ship for the Spanish Netherlands. A

*   Rochester is in fact more than 20 miles from Eltham.

number of horses, mules, hounds and greyhounds also joined the party. The gentlewomen, who became in effect Jane's ladies-in-waiting, included her cousin Margaret Harrington, Eleanor Paston, two daughters of Sir Thomas Stradling and Susan Clarencius, who travelled with her woman, four serving men and two horses. Jane's grandmother, Lady Dormer, also went with them, together with two gentlemen, four serving men and a chaplain. Jane's uncle, Sir Henry Sidney, came to Dover to say goodbye.

Having landed at Calais, where she was greeted by the governor and rested for two nights, Jane and her party continued to Dunkirk and Newport. Chaloner reported to Cecil that she had been 'princely met upon the way and would rest her in a Spaniard's house in Bruges'. There she was received by members of the court of the Duchess of Parma, illegitimate daughter of Charles V. She had just been appointed Governor of the Netherlands by her half-brother Philip, who was on the point of returning to Spain. According to the Venetian ambassador at Philip's court, Feria hoped 'to obtain leave from his Majesty to remain to keep [the Countess] company and should he have to cross over to Spain, he will return immediately, which determination displeases the Duchess of Parma, who knows that if he remains here he will have a great share in the government of these Provinces'. Feria seems to have had a talent for putting people's backs up, but the arrival of Chaloner in Flanders, albeit as Elizabeth's representative in the country, had a calming effect on the situation following Philip's departure. Unlike many Englishmen at Elizabeth's court, Chaloner was not ill-disposed towards Feria,* and he later became a good friend of Jane's in Spain. He also got on well with Cecil, after he had been sent to meet the new Holy Roman Emperor, Ferdinand I, to sound him out on the subject of a possible marriage between Elizabeth and one of the Emperor's sons. Chaloner's first posting as ambassador was to Flanders, where he remained for seven months, and after a spell back in England he departed reluctantly to Spain, 'that land of heat and Inquisition', as ambassador at Philip's court in Madrid. He arrived, via Paris and Bilbao, in the spring of 1562 and stayed in post until 1565, the year that he died.

---

* They were the same age, and they may both have been on Charles V's failed expedition to Algiers against Barbary pirates in 1541. Chaloner was one of four Englishmen who accompanied the Emperor.

Jane and her retinue continued their journey to Ghent and Antwerp, where they were welcomed by the governors of the town with a military salute and 'discharging of all the artillery of the place', before taking the road south. From some miles away she would have seen the great tower of Mechlin (in French, Malines) cathedral rising more than 300 feet above the Flanders plain. As they entered the city in the first week of August, crossing the 13th-century stone bridge over the river Dyle, the party of English Catholics passed the cathedral before turning towards the palaces of the three Margarets. On one side is the palace lived in by Margaret of York until she died in 1503. A granddaughter of John of Gaunt, and sister of Edward IV and Richard III, she married Charles the Bold, Duke of Burgundy, in a union against France. Charles made Mechlin the administrative capital of the Burgundian Low Countries, and after his death on the battlefield in 1477, Margaret moved to this palace which had been built by the Bishop of Cambrai, illegitimate son of Charles the Bold's grandfather. (Today this unprepossessing building, the Stadsschouwburg, is used as a theatre.)

Opposite Margaret of York's palace stands the rather more imposing red-brick residence, step-gabled with rows of arches and columns, of her goddaughter and step-granddaughter, Margaret of Austria, which she built in 1507 and where the Countess had come to stay. By the time she was 24, Margaret of Austria had been widowed twice. She vowed never to marry again after the death of her second husband, Philibert Duke of Savoy, but was appointed governor of the Low Countries by her father, Maximilian, Holy Roman Emperor, who tried to persuade her to marry Henry VII. She remained at Mechlin until her death in 1530, ruling on behalf of her nephew Charles, whose father Philip I was her brother and whose mother, Juana, was the sister of Juan, to whom Margaret had been briefly married.

All sorts of interesting people were received at Margaret's court—Thomas More, Erasmus, Albrecht Dürer—and the 12-year-old Anne Boleyn spent 18 months there as a member of Margaret's household, where she was affectionately known as 'la petite Boulin'. Having been born in Ghent, Charles (to become Emperor Charles V) spent much of his childhood at Margaret of York's palace, flying kites and learning to shoot with a crossbow, supervised from across the street by his aunt Margaret in the Court of Savoy, as her palace was known. His father died when he was six and his mother

Juana remained in Spain. Charles was betrothed a year later to Mary Tudor, Henry VIII's sister, but she married the widowed Louis XII of France. Three of Charles's sisters were also raised by their aunt, including Mary 'of Hungary', who succeeded Margaret as governor in 1530. When Margaret died, her body was taken to be buried alongside her husband Philibert in the monastery of Brou, which she had built in his memory at Bourg-en-Bresse, capital of the dukes of Savoy. Two hundred years later her viscera were interred beneath the altar of the church of Sts Peter and Paul opposite her palace in Mechlin.

The early 16th century had been Mechlin's 'golden age' of commercial and political importance—by the 1513 Treaty of Mechlin a European alliance was formed against France—but it declined during Mary's governorship, principally because she spent most of her time living at Coudenberg, a palace in Brussels. However, the city enjoyed a revival in 1559 thanks to Philip who, before he left Flushing for Spain in August, decreed that Mechlin should be the religious capital of Flanders and appointed Cardinal de Granvelle* as its first archbishop. The Countess of Feria now arrived to stay with the third Margaret of Mechlin, Duchess of Parma.

Margaret of Parma had been brought up in Mechlin, under the supervision of the two previous governors, before being sent to Italy where she was married to a Medici who was assassinated the following year. A marriage to Ottavio Farnese, Duke of Parma, came next, but she returned to the Netherlands without him some 15 years later, where she was appointed governor in August 1559 by her half-brother Philip. It was said of Margaret that the only feminine thing about her was her sex, and that in her woman's dress she gave the impression of a man in petticoats. She had the misfortune to have hair growing on her face and she suffered from gout; but she was politically astute and rigorously Catholic, having had Ignatius Loyola as her confessor in her early years. Both her half-brother John of Austria, who led the Holy Alliance to defeat the Ottoman Turks at the Battle of Lepanto, and her son Alessandro Farnese were famous military commanders.

Chaloner had an audience with the Duchess of Parma shortly after his

---

* His appointment was confirmed by Pope Pius IV in 1561 and he took his seat as archbishop at the end of that year. He had assisted Charles V's ambassador, Simon Renard, in the negotiations for Philip's marriage to Mary in 1554.

arrival, but the King did not immediately agree to receive him, after Feria had complained of Elizabeth's supposed 'ill-usage' of his wife before she left England. The meeting was finally arranged by Feria after the King had attended three days of celebrations with the Knights of the Order of the Golden Fleece, which had been founded in Bruges in the previous century. Chaloner watched the King in procession, 'all clad in robes of the Order.... very rich and fair to behold'. Once the rituals were over, he reported to the Queen, Philip received him 'clad in a plain black cloak with cloth cap (for he mourneth) very plainly'—in homage to his late father, one suspects, rather than to his late wife.

While Philip was waiting to embark at Flushing for his voyage to Spain, Elizabeth was issuing instructions that, should his ship be driven by winds on to the English coast, he should be given every assistance; 'to our said good brother that honour that to so great a Prince apperteineth and to one with whom we be assured in firm and perfect amity'. Margaret of Parma, Chaloner, Feria and various nobles went to Flushing to say their farewells, but he did not sail until the last week of August, with a favourable east wind. Chaloner counted the King's fleet: 20 Spanish ships, 30 Flemish, and 40 'of others of less sort'. After an uneventful voyage the fleet put into the port of Laredo, between Santander and Bilbao, on 8th September and Philip arrived in Valladolid a week later.

Margaret of Parma's regency of the Netherlands was conducted between Brussels, Ghent and Mechlin, and as the time approached for Jane to give birth, the Duchess spent much of the time at her Mechlin residence. She wanted not only to keep an eye on the health of her guest but also on the Count of Feria, fearing his interference in affairs of state. Communication with Margaret of Parma may not have been easy, as her preferred language was Italian, but the 21-year-old Jane also had two older and experienced Englishwomen, Susan Clarencius, who was about 50, and her grandmother Lady Dormer, to look after her.

Before he left Flanders, the King instructed his envoy, Don Antonio de Toledo, the Duke of Alba's brother, to visit Jane on his behalf, which he did, accompanied by 40 'gentlemen'. 'Much honour is done here unto her,' Chaloner commented to Cecil, a month before she was due to give birth. When the time came, it was not an easy birth: Chaloner reported to Cecil on 29th September that 'the Countess of Feria is brought to bed at Mechlin of a boy, with much joy of the Count. She had a long travail.' She was fortunate, however, to be attended by the distinguished local physician and botanist, Rembert Dodoens, who had turned down the offer of court physician to Philip II. Feria reported the birth to Quadra in London, but Jane's health continued to give concern. 'The Countess is still sadly ailing but the boy is well... I have the Antwerp physician here who I hope to God will cure her... We cannot leave here until after the winter cold is over,' Feria wrote to Quadra. It was not until mid-November, when she was judged to be out of danger, that Chaloner congratulated Feria and informed Elizabeth. But he may have been exaggerating when he wrote that 'the Countess, through her dangerous travail in childbirth and evil handling of the midwives, has ever since been very weak, as her life was despaired of'. The Queen replied promptly to Chaloner, asking him to pass on to Jane her 'hartye commendations, and declaring that we have willed you to do so'. Meanwhile, as she recovered her strength, Jane was able to leave her baby in the care of Susan Clarencius who, according to Feria, was 'wonderfully attentive'. The child was christened Lorenzo and among his godparents were Margaret of Parma and Cardinal de Granvelle, who had just been appointed her chief councillor.

Elizabeth's interest in Jane's well-being may have been no more than one woman's concern for another who had been seven months' pregnant when they last met. But it is clear from Chaloner's communications with Cecil that the Queen wished her well. Despite their religious differences, and the fact that the Queen resented Jane's husband's continuing interference in her affairs of state and the heart, she did not forget that Jane had served her half-sister loyally until her death. And now one of Elizabeth's favourite ladies-in-waiting was Mary Sidney, sister of Robert Dudley and married to Jane's uncle.

However, Feria was trying the patience of Elizabeth's ambassador in Flanders. They dined together on one or two occasions and Chaloner was introduced to the baby. But he was embarrassed by Feria speaking openly of 'the most secret things of the state of England' and of his well-founded opinion of what was happening 'about the Queen her Grace's person'. Much to Elizabeth's annoyance, Chaloner reported back to her that Feria 'lamented that your Majesty gave not your mind to marriage… He verily supposeth your Grace is not determined to marry at all.' In January 1560 Chaloner wrote to tell Cecil that 'the Count of Feria with his lady depart hence for Spain on the 20th of the next [month] by easy journeys through France. I would he were gone.'

Another reason for Chaloner's irritation was Feria's insistent demand for a licence for Susan Clarencius and Jane's grandmother to remain out of England. As English subjects, they were required to have a licence to travel abroad, and had applied for passports before leaving England, not only for themselves but, in Lady Dormer's case, for 'two gentlewomen, four serving men and a chaplain', and for Mrs Clarencius 'her woman, four serving men and two horses'. Although they were safely out of the country, their property and assets in England were at risk of being seized. Susan Clarencius had set up a trust fund for her nephews before she left England, and Lady Dormer wanted to transfer 20,000 ducats to her granddaughter before it was confiscated by the Privy Council and handed to her son. (Feria was semi-permanently in debt and the money would be needed for their journey to Spain. He was able to borrow 50,000 ducats from an Italian banker in Antwerp.) It seems that Elizabeth had initially refused Feria's request to grant a licence, saying that 'the Spanish court is the asylum for all our enemies'. But he persisted, writing to Quadra repeatedly to ask him to pursue the matter, with Dudley and Mary Sidney, but without asking Cecil who was likely to be obstructive: 'that knave Cecil will certainly try some roguish trick'. It is not clear when or if the question of the licence was finally resolved. But in March 1560, as the Ferias prepared to leave Flanders, Elizabeth's envoy in Brussels, Sir John Legh, was telling her: 'The Count of Feria takes great unkindness that the Queen denied him licence for the Lady Dormer's longer tarrying here, and for Clarencius' going into Spain, and said he heard the cause was that the Queen was informed that he would misreport her.' Towards the end of 1560, when the question was largely academic, Elizabeth was apparently still refusing to issue the licences because, as she wrote to Philip, it might lead to results prejudicial to the realm. However, as a token of her goodwill towards the Countess of Feria, she stated that 'if they will return and live quietly they will have her favour'. Neither of them returned and the matter was dropped.

While Feria had no proper job in Flanders and kept telling Chaloner of his frustration at Elizabeth's behaviour, he was also complaining about Philip to Quadra, his successor in London.

'...in truth every time I recollect how the King has gone to Spain without making proper provision for your lordship, I am so annoyed that I cannot help expressing it. I do not wish to recount the way his Majesty treated matters during the last few weeks he was here. He cared little whether we paid out of our own pockets... I hope he will open his eyes now that he has gone to cure his homesickness in Spain. Things are going badly there...'

When Feria heard that Elizabeth had been accusing Jane of speaking out against her, he rushed to her defence and fired off an angry letter to Quadra in London:

'The Queen has no right to complain of my wife for having spoken about her for really she has been most reticent and has never said a word. I believe I am the culprit for saying what I know to be true, and the Queen will repent of having behaved as she has to me before a year is over.'

Quadra was much more of a diplomat than Feria. He was better at dealing with Elizabeth than Feria had been, but on occasion she drove him almost to despair, writing to Feria that 'With her all is falsehood and vanity... I think [she] must have 100,000 devils in her body, notwithstanding that she is for ever telling me that she yearns to be a nun and to pass her time in a cell praying.'

As the time approached for the Ferias' departure from Mechlin and preparations were made for their long journey to Spain with their infant son, correspondence with Quadra was temporarily suspended, and Chaloner had to listen to fewer outbursts against Elizabeth. Although Chaloner understood that the Ferias would be leaving Flanders on 20th February, and he was counting the days, they stayed for another month while Jane continued her recovery. In Mechlin, when Jane felt well enough to leave the Court of Savoy where she was staying, she would have walked the short distance to the main square, past flat-fronted wooden houses pressed together, some of them surmounted by turrets and sculpted figures. As the narrow street opened out, there was the magnificent cathedral dedicated to St Rumbold, an Irish evangelist responsible for converting the city to Christianity in the 8th century. Within, she was confronted by the cavernous nave, pillared and vaulted, where she lit an offertory candle and prayed for the health of her son during the long journey ahead, Jane may also have worshipped at St Janskerk, a 15th-century Gothic church of the two Johns (Baptist and Evangelist). It is likely, too, that she visited the Benedictine abbots at their House of Refuge in St Trond's Abbey, and the widows, spinsters and orphans residing at the beguinages close to the city walls.

Before they left Mechlin, Jane wanted to see her grandmother safely and comfortably housed in Louvain, where she would spend the rest of her life. This town, founded in the 9th century, was the home of the Counts of Louvain, one of whom had a daughter, Adeliza, who became queen of England as Henry I's second wife. Louvain was an important centre of cloth manufacture before the oldest and most prominent university in the Netherlands was founded there in the 15th century. Thomas More's seminal work, *Utopia*, was first published in Louvain and the town attracted a number of exiled English Catholics, among whom Lady Dormer was a leading light and spent much of her time. She did attempt once to return to England to collect rents due to her, but the Queen gave orders that she should not be allowed to land. Feria was apparently so angry at this petty interference that, against his wife's advice, he tried to get the Pope to excommunicate Elizabeth. When Lady Dormer died in 1571, aged 84, her funeral was attended by many residents of local monasteries and the town's poor to whom she had given and bequeathed alms. Her granddaughter Jane had a marble tomb erected in her memory in the charterhouse in Louvain, and paid an annual sum of 100 florins for its upkeep. The Carthusian monastery was largely destroyed by Napoleon's troops, who used it as an ammunition depot, and further damage was caused during both world wars. The university library was destroyed in 1914 and thousands of books were lost, though the magnificently ornate town hall survived. Today the buildings which stand on the site of the monastery belong to the university and have been converted to house children in care. Nothing remains of the old 15th-century charterhouse.

Jane's elder sister Anne, whose husband Sir Walter Hungerford had been imprisoned following their divorce, came to Louvain in 1571 to see her grandmother before she died. It seems that Jane had persuaded Robert Dudley, now Earl of Leicester, to issue a temporary licence for her sister to come to Flanders, but Anne stayed on and took over Lady Dormer's house-hold after her death. Although she was granted a pension from Philip, she received no funds from England and wrote frequently to ask her sister for help. She died at Louvain in 1603 and was buried next to her grandmother.

IV

A new friend in France

THE FERIAS, their baby son and Jane's gentlewomen, together with a number of attendants, finally left Mechlin in the middle of March. They had first to take leave of their hostess, Margaret of Parma, who was waiting in Brussels to receive them and say goodbye. It must have been quite a send-off: Sir John Legh reported to the Queen that this stately procession was joined some distance from Brussels by 'above 200 horse, amongst whom were the Bishop of Arras [*aka* Cardinal de Granvelle], divers of the Council, and all the nobility of the Court'. For two or three days the Ferias lodged with the Regent, and 'dined and supped continuously' with her, though she regretted that there was 'too little time to entertain the Countess and Don Lorenzo her son'.

From Brussels the almost regal caravan made its way via Mons, Saint-Quentin and Compiegne to Paris, where the Ferias stayed over Easter with the Duke of Guise. Jane's former royal mistress, Mary, would not have approved of her supping with the man who had led French troops to capture Calais less than a year before her death. But he was also the uncle of Mary Stuart (daughter of James V of Scotland and Mary of Guise), who was now married to Francis, king of France; and the Ferias were going on to meet the royal teenagers at the Château d'Amboise on the river Loire.* In fact the Duke may not have been in Paris to welcome the Ferias, as he and his brother, the Cardinal of Lorraine, who represented much of the power behind the throne (after the Regent, Francis's mother, Catherine de Medici), had just put down a Huguenot conspiracy at Amboise to overthrow the King. Unaware of these goings-on, the Ferias continued their journey by

---

* Leonardo da Vinci spent the last three years of his life in Amboise, and was buried in the collegiate church of the château.

way of Chartres, Orleans and Blois, to Amboise, arriving towards the end of April, only a month after Protestant corpses had been hanging from the walls of the château. Francis and Mary, who had taken refuge at Catherine de Medici's château at Chenonceau, came to Amboise to meet their guests.

The King and Queen of France were 16 and 17 respectively; Francis's father, Henri II, had proclaimed them king and queen of England before his death; and Mary had been queen of Scotland since she was six days old. Born in 1542, Mary was betrothed to Henry VIII's son Edward before her first birthday, but the Scottish parliament rejected the match and instead agreed to a French marriage treaty. Since Mary, now aged five, was in danger of being kidnapped by the English, her French mother agreed that she should be raised in France. She remained at the French court for the next 13 years, marrying the Dauphin Francis in 1558, who became king just over a year later. At the time of the Ferias' visit, Francis, who was physically feeble and deformed, would have only another seven months to live; Mary returned to Scotland, probably still a virgin, the following year. Her mother, Mary of Guise, queen regent of Scotland, was on her deathbed while the Ferias were at Amboise.

While Jane was not of royal blood, the trust and affection between her and Mary Tudor, and the potential importance of her role as English Catholic exile in the confidence, through her husband, of the King of Spain, made her a useful ally in Mary's ambition to replace Elizabeth on the English throne. But what was anticipated initially as a political relationship became almost at once a close friendship between the French queen and the 22-year-old Jane. According to Jane's biographer, Henry Clifford, as soon as they met Mary admired her guest's 'beauty, the sweetness of her countenance and the good grace of her person... and was marvellously taken with her presence, and showered affection for her.' Mary had been wearing black, in mourning for the death of her father-in-law, but in Jane's honour she dressed in white. She then invited Jane

> 'to be apparelled after the French manner, which, to please the Queen, she yielded to; and the Queen would have her clothed in her presence, which her Majesty did put her hand to, taking in it very particular content, for she would mend what the women had done; and from that time the Queen began to bear her so entire and intimate love as she continued to keep it to her death.'

Assuming the role of lady-in-waiting, Mary enjoyed dressing Jane, who regularly ate at Mary's table, was waited on by 'the guard of the Scots gentlemen' and generally treated as if she were a near-equal, a royal princess. While Mary was being brought up at the French court, her future sister-in-law, Elizabeth of Valois, became her closest friend. After Elizabeth had been sent away to Spain to become Philip II's third wife, it is reasonable to think that Mary latched on to Jane as a replacement for the French princess in her affections. The Ferias stayed at Amboise for no more than a week, but Mary and Jane exchanged letters and gifts for much of the rest of Mary's life.

The Venetian ambassador reported that Mary gave Jane 'two very handsome gowns, one of cloth of gold with a raised pile, the other of crimson satin covered with golden embroidery, and a jewelled ornament for the neck, the entire present being considered of great value'. The suggestion was that Mary made these gifts because she was so upset at Jane's treatment by Elizabeth when she left England. However, Mary was unlikely to have been aware of the incident unless Feria gave her his version of it, no doubt trenchantly expressing his opinion of the English queen.

Feria was also unofficially playing politics on his master's behalf. He knew that Philip would not want Mary to replace Elizabeth on the English throne while she was queen of France, as the powerful influence of the Guises would then extend to England. However, after the deaths of Mary's mother and then Francis during 1560, the threat which Philip feared was removed. He was, of course, now married to Francis's sister, Elizabeth of Valois—and Feria assured Francis that he would do his utmost to persuade Philip to ally himself formally with France against Elizabeth. But neither the marriage (she died in 1568) nor the Franco-Spanish friendship was going to last.

The King and Queen of France extended their hospitality to several Englishmen and women during the few days the Ferias spent at Amboise. Apart from the ladies attending Jane, and Susan Clarencius, who had the care of her infant son Lorenzo, there was Sir Richard Shelley, a Knight of St John (he would become grand prior) and a diplomat, on occasion in the service of Philip of Spain. He had escorted Mary of Guise in 1551 when she returned to Scotland from France, and was now accompanying the Ferias on their journey through France. At Amboise he was received by Sir

Nicholas Throckmorton, Elizabeth's ambassador to France, and asked him
to tell the Queen that, in spite of his years spent in Catholic Europe, he
remained her faithful subject. Another English recusant and a Knight of
Malta, Sir Oliver Starkey, was also present at Amboise in the Ferias' party
and protesting his loyalty to Elizabeth.

The presence of Throckmorton at Amboise must have been embarrassing
both to him and to the English Catholic coterie staying at the French king's
court. He was committed to the Protestant, and in France to the Huguenot,
cause, and during his career was imprisoned four times, both by the English
and French authorities. Having been suspected of complicity in Wyatt's
rebellion in 1554 he was sent to the Tower by Queen Mary, but successfully
defended himself on the charge of treason. While in France, Throckmorton
urged Elizabeth to send an army to join the Huguenots and act as champion
of the reformed faith. At the same time he was impressed by Mary Stuart
and was on good terms with her, in spite of their religious differences; they
continued to exchange letters for some years.

At the end of 1560, following the death of Mary's husband Francis,
Throckmorton was writing back to England that she had

> 'both a great wisdom for her years, modesty, and also great judgment in
> the wise handling [of] herself and her matters, which, increasing with her
> years, cannot but turn greatly to her commendation, reputation, honour
> and great benefit of her and her country... I see her behaviour to be such,
> and her wisdom and kingly modesty so great, in that she thinketh herself
> not too wise, but is content to be ruled by good counsel and wise men
> (which is a great virtue in a prince or princess, and which argueth a great
> judgment and wisdom in her).'

Throckmorton was not only paying compliments to Mary but comparing
her favourably with his queen's unwise behaviour towards Robert Dudley,
whose wife had just been found dead in possibly suspicious circumstances
and who, according to rumour, was about to become Elizabeth's husband.
However, Mary's judgment and wisdom failed her when she took up with
Lord Darnley. Elizabeth sent Throckmorton to Scotland charged with per-
suading Mary not to marry Darnley and to accept Dudley (now Earl of
Leicester) as a suitor instead, but his mission was unsuccessful. Years later
she sent Throckmorton north again to attempt to secure Mary's release from

imprisonment by Protestant Scottish nobles. Then he was briefly imprisoned in the Tower for having acted in Mary's cause by recommending that
she marry the Duke of Norfolk. Throckmorton died in 1571, some years
before his cousin Francis was involved in a plot (which carried his name)
to put Mary on the English throne, with help from France and Spain. She
may or may not have been party to the conspiracy, but Francis implicated
her before he was executed. The Protestant Sir Nicholas Throckmorton was
a better friend to Mary than the Catholic Francis.

Forty-four years old when she died, Mary was still a teenager when the
Ferias lodged with her at Amboise; and when they left at the beginning of
May to continue their journey south, she would never see her new friend
Jane again. But each would offer to help the other in the years ahead. At
the time of Mary's abdication in favour of her one-year-old son James, Jane
instructed her husband to send her 20,000 ducats, which they could ill
afford. In 1571 Mary, now under house arrest in England, tried to persuade
Jane to leave Spain following her husband's death and move to Flanders,
no doubt hoping to see her again. She wrote both to Philip and to Pope
Pius V, urging Jane's appointment as Governor of the Netherlands. Mary
sent her friend 'a book of gold with the old service in Latin', adding, in her
own hand, 'Absit nobis gloriari, nisi in cruce Domini nostri Jesu Christi.
Marie R.' (God forbid that we should glory, save in the cross of our Lord
Jesus Christ.) In her letters to Jane, Mary was in the habit of signing herself
'your perfect friend, old acquaintance, & dear cousin'. Jane can hardly have
approved Mary's choice of husbands in Scotland, nor of her sometimes
impulsive and ill-judged behaviour, but she always sympathised with her
plight and the friendship only ended with Mary's death.

The Ferias' route south from Amboise would have taken them via Tours,
Poitiers, Bordeaux and Bayonne to the Spanish border at Irun. A number
of wagons, muleteers and a baggage train accompanied the convoy, with
servants going ahead, with the Ferias' furniture, to prepare lodging for each
night. This was often at a monastery or perhaps a castle owned by a member
of the royal family entourage who would have been alerted by Francis and
Mary. In both France and Spain some of the best roads, or at least the
straightest tracks, in the 16th century were built by the clergy and led to
their monasteries. As for the modes of transport, four-wheeled carriages

were something of a novelty, and used mainly in northern Europe. (One of the first in England was built for the Earl of Rutland by Walter Rippon of York in 1555.) They were not suitable for use in mountainous country or on steep hills. When Margaret of Austria set out from the port of Santander to travel to Burgos to marry Queen Isabella's son Juan in 1497, she and her Burgundian party soon found that the only way to cross the Cantabrian mountains was by mule, and the carriages had to be abandoned. Isabella's daughter Juana left Flanders four years later with her husband and 100 carriages and wagons, and had the same experience when they began to climb the hills on tracks covered with ice in January. Mules took them through the mountain passes, though it is recorded that one carriage struggled through the Basque country and astounded the local people who had never seen such a conveyance before. When Sir Thomas Chamberlain was returning to England from his posting as ambassador in Madrid in 1562, he wrote from Bayonne in March that he found 'such crooked ways for his waggon and such deep ones for his horse that he has not been able to make four leagues [about 12 miles] a day'.

Having travelled through the flat country of the Landes to Bayonne and then across the border to San Sebastian, the Ferias headed south-west to Burgos and east of the Cantabrian mountains. The road through the Basque region to Vitoria rises to about 1,800 feet above sea level: even in June carriages would have been difficult for the horses to pull, in country with a high rainfall, and many preferred to transfer from four wheels to four legs. However, the passengers in carriages would have had a less uncomfortable ride than in the previous century. It was in the late 1400s that a lighter, faster carriage was developed in Hungary with suspension, using either chains or leather braces. (The name 'coach' may have come from the post-town of Kocs between Budapest and Vienna.) The Holy Roman Emperor Charles V was known to favour this new type of transport, in which he travelled regularly until he was persuaded, because of his gout and other infirmities, to be conveyed by litter. Presumably, when the going became too rough, Jane's eight-month-old son Lorenzo would have been transferred to a litter for short distances rather than risked on the back of a mule in the arms of Mistress Clarencius, who was now in her 50s. While the discomfort and dangers of this journey through 16th-century Spain on stony, rutted tracks may seem almost insupportable to cosseted 21st-century travellers, there was no other way of getting over land from A to B, however distant. Teresa of Avila, approaching 60 years old, was riding all over Spain at this time and sleeping rough.

There is no record of the Ferias' progress through Spain, but it is safe to assume that, while passing through Burgos, they would have visited the convent of Las Huelgas outside the city, which was founded in the 12th century by Eleanor of England, daughter of Henry II, who became queen of Castile by marrying Alfonso VIII. She and her husband were buried in the convent where, 40 years later, Eleanor of Castile married the future Edward I. The Ferias' route continued to Valladolid, and then by the pilgrims' path, the Camino del Sureste, towards Toledo, which we know they reached on 9th August. This camino would have taken them via Tordesillas, where Charles V's mother Juana (known as *Juana la Loca*, Joan the Mad) was effectively incarcerated for the last 30 years of her life. She had died five years earlier, in 1555. The next town reached on the way south was Medina del Campo, a name which would have resonated with Jane. It was here, in 1489, that a treaty was signed to agree the marriage of Catherine of Aragon (mother of Jane's former mistress Mary) to Henry VII's son Arthur. The Ferias would probably have lodged either in the castle at Madrigal de las Altas Torres, where Juana's and Catherine's mother Isabella was born, or the castle of Arévalo, where Isabella spent much of her childhood. This region of Castile is filled with the history of 15th- and 16th-century Spain. (Jane's 17th-century biographer Henry Clifford mentions that the convoy made a diversion to Segovia in order to meet Philip and his French wife Elizabeth, who were not there. It is more likely that a messenger was dispatched to Segovia, only to learn that the royal couple were at Toledo, where the court resided.) Having climbed to the city of Avila, at 3,700 feet, and admired its great walls, the Ferias' descent through the lower slopes of the Sierra de Gredos took them to Toros de Guisando, famous for its four Iron Age granite bulls and for the treaty, in 1468, which recognised the 17-year-old Isabella as heir presumptive to the crown of Castile.

Jane's arrival in Toledo was greeted as if she were a visiting queen. 'The houses of the city were dispeopled to behold her entrance.' Clifford describes the King and Feria, who must have gone on ahead, standing 'together in a window to see her pass, she riding on horseback; the furniture of her horse being of crimson velvet garnished with studs and richly appointed. Her six dames likewise were all alone on horseback, with velvet furniture, suitable alike. The Duchess [sic] had attending on her 20 pages, all in costly liveries, and was accompanied with most of the gallantry of the court. But her own person graced all. The King, before she visited the Queen, came himself to see her, to bid her welcome to the court of Spain.'

After a journey from Amboise of around 1,000 miles and taking three months, Jane and her entourage must surely have rested a while and had access to suitable gowns and other apparel, not to mention coiffeurs, before making this grand entrance into Toledo when, at the beginning of August, the temperature would have been uncomfortably hot—rising to at least 30°C during the day. Jane hadn't seen Philip for three years, when he had left England and his wife Mary for the last time. As the only Englishwoman to have formed an alliance with a confidant of the Spanish king during Philip's time in England, Jane was a useful contact and informant for Philip in his relations with and understanding of Elizabeth. There were times when Jane would intervene to check her husband's instinctive hostility to Elizabeth, whom he once referred to as *esa Medea* (that Medea). For the moment Philip was pleased to see her as the happy legacy of his otherwise forgettable years as nominal king of England.

The next day Jane was taken to meet Philip's third wife, Elizabeth of Valois, whom Feria had escorted to Spain the previous year following the Peace of Cateau-Cambrésis between France and Spain and her proxy wedding in Paris. Elizabeth received Jane 'with much show of kindness and favour, as much admiring her beauty as envying her nation; and she gave her a jewel for her welcome,' according to Clifford's account. Jane would have known how close a friendship Elizabeth had formed with her sister-in-law, and she had much to tell of Mary's kindness to her. At the same time Elizabeth was well aware of her brother Francis's poor health and of the probability that she would not see him again. Elizabeth, having married Philip the previous year aged 14, bore him two daughters before she died in childbirth at the age of 23. She had originally been betrothed to Philip's son Carlos, which fact was transformed into two largely fictional accounts—a play by Schiller, and one of Verdi's greatest operas.

Henry Clifford was, of course, indulging in a measure of hyperbole when he wrote that 'the report of her virtue and the comeliness of her presence drew a regard and honour to her of the whole court, by all performances, in such noble and extraordinary manner as the memory thereof remains much extolled'. But there is no doubt that she made quite a hit in Toledo during the few days that the Ferias stayed at court. The King of Portugal, who was passing through, invited Jane to visit his country and presented her with a jewel valued at 8,000 ducats.

The English ambassador at Philip's court, present in Toledo for the Ferias' visit, was Sir Thomas Chamberlain. He had been ambassador in Flanders during Mary of Hungary's regency, and was appointed by Elizabeth to Spain at the beginning of 1560. But he was not a happy man either in Toledo or Madrid, to which the court moved the following year. The climate did not suit him, and nor did the cost of living. His predecessor told Cecil that unless Chamberlain was given more money the Queen's service would suffer; and he wrote that he had 'so far stretched his poor ability to advance this service'. When Chamberlain left Spain in 1562, he also left a mountain of debt, and was fortunate that he had a friend in Feria, who helped him reach an accommodation with at least some of his creditors. His other problem had been with his cook, who was arrested by the Inquisition for possessing heretical books. Diplomatic privilege was invoked, Feria interceded with Philip on the cook's behalf, and the matter was dropped, though not before Feria informed Chamberlain that the jurisdiction of the Inquisition was paramount. When Sir Thomas Chaloner came to replace Chamberlain as ambassador in 1562, he was not best pleased to find his predecessor still in the embassy. He left behind some leather hangings and a quantity of plate which, at considerable inconvenience and cost, were returned to Chamberlain in England.

Jane and her husband had a few days of rest and recuperation, enjoying the no doubt generous hospitality of Philip's court, and had the opportunity to worship in Toledo's great Gothic cathedral, which had been completed some 70 years earlier. El Greco had yet to arrive in the city where he painted most of his best work, having failed to find favour with Philip. When the Ferias set off again, on the last leg of their journey to Zafra in Extremadura, it would have taken them two or three weeks to cover the distance which,

A 17th c. view of Zafra by Israël Silvestre, showing the Feria castle in the centre and the convent of Santa Marina on the left.

even on today's direct roads, is almost 200 miles—though Henry Clifford implies that they reached their destination in a matter of days. The party would probably have followed the course of the river Tagus to Talavera de la Reina (where Wellington would win his first victory in Spain 250 years later against the forces of Napoleon), then continued to Oropesa and the evocatively named Navalmoral de la Mata, before joining the Via de la Plata to Caceres. From Caceres their route would have taken them due south on the ancient Roman road to the city of Merida, once the capital of Lusitania, where they would have crossed the Roman bridge and admired the Roman theatre and the Temple of Diana. Richard Ford described this commercial way between Salamanca and Merida as the Queen of Roads, and its old stone pavement may have provided easier travelling conditions for the Feria party. But it was still high summer, with temperatures in Extremadura usually around 35°C. After Merida they continued on the same road (today the main highway is called the Autovia Ruta de la Plata), through Almendralejo and past the village of Feria to Zafra.

No sooner had they arrived in Zafra than Feria was writing to Cardinal de Granvelle (recently appointed Archbishop of Mechlin) to complain about the weather. Philip had already expressed a wish to go back to the Low Countries, and now Feria, with his talent for hyperbole, wrote:

> 'Spain is the most backward province on the face of the earth, and devil take me if I don't round up half of all I have and return to Flanders. Besides which, my wife pleads with me every day to go back and has not had a good day's health since she came.'

But they stayed, the temperature was more bearable in winter and Jane learnt to adapt to the summer heat by staying in the shade within the thick castle walls. In the cooler evening air she sometimes climbed the steps to the roof, where from the battlements she could look down past the Convent of Santa Marina to the Convent of Santa Clara, where previous Counts of Feria were buried, and beyond to the Church of La Candelaria. The church was still under construction, having been started when Feria was a boy, and was being continued now that he had returned to Zafra with his English wife. Collegiate status for this grand church was sought by their son towards the end of the century, and was granted by the Pope shortly before Jane's death. An imposing altarpiece was then added—some of it may have been the work of the Extremaduran artist, Francisco de Zurbaran—and much later the red-brick bell tower.

In the mid-16th century the family seat consisted of a baronial residence within a fortress which had been built by the lord of Feria—he became the first count—more than 100 years earlier. (Until then he had been living at the Hospital de Santiago, which he founded for the town's poor and sick.) Permission to construct the castle on the site of a Moorish alcázar was given by the then king of Castile, Juan II, whose mother was Catherine of Lancaster, daughter of John of Gaunt. Some years earlier Gomez Suarez de Figueroa, a Master of the Order of Santiago in recognition of military successes against the Arab invaders, built a castle on a hill above the small town of Feria, a few miles north-west of Zafra. The castle, on the site of a Roman fort, which preceded an 11th-century Moorish fort, commands a panoramic view over the surrounding country. Today it still has its central 'homage' tower (*torre de homenaje*) about 40 metres high, its medieval parade ground and a modern museum. In the town the five fig-leaves of the Ferias' coat of arms are sculpted into the concrete paving of the main square.

The fig-leaves are also to be seen on the façade of the castle in Zafra, also with its central cylindrical keep. The building was converted to an Italianate Renaissance palace towards the end of the 16th century, principally by the Ferias' son Lorenzo, who added a courtyard of white, veined marble, with a central fountain, surrounded by two storeys of arches and Doric pilasters. A wide staircase leads to rooms with coffered ceilings of gilded polychrome wood and a Mudejar chapel with octagonal cupola. In later centuries, after the Suarez de Figueroa line was extinguished, the palace was used variously as tax offices, telegraph offices, and Zafra's first secondary school. In the Civil War it became a hospital and prison, and later housed destitute families. In 1968 the castle was opened as a state-run hotel (*parador*) and called after Hernan Cortes, who spent time in Zafra as a teenager before sailing for Hispaniola in 1504.

The Suarez de Figueroa family owned extensive estates which not only incorporated the town of Zafra but also a number of pueblos nearby, some of them fortified to repel incursions from Portugal, which often led to the plundering of Portuguese border towns. Among the castles of the Feria estate is the Castillo de los Arcos, near Almendral on the road to Portugal, built by the nephew of the 1st Count of Feria in the 1470s. It is an impressive fortress, with four crenellated towers, battlements and embrasures for the cannons which were fired on the hapless Portuguese below. A similar construction, of the same period, stands in the nearby village of Nogales, with a *torre de homenaje* within the walls. Both castles acknowledge their founder, with the Feria fig-leaves incised in the masonry. The 15th-century counts of Feria were involved not only in border battles with the Portuguese but in the war of the Castilian succession between two women, Isabella, married to Ferdinand of Aragon and Joanna *La Beltraneja*, married to the king of Portugal. More than three centuries later, during the Peninsular War, the bloody battle of La Albuera was fought only a few miles away, when more than 12,000 were killed in a single day. 'Oh Albuera, glorious field of grief!' Byron wrote in *Childe Harold's Pilgrimage*. This is also the country of the great bustard, the heaviest flying bird in the world. Spain's population of this magnificent bird is estimated at more than 30,000, about two thirds of the total number worldwide, and a large proportion of them live on what used to be Feria land. On these plains of lower Extremadura the great bustards can be seen wandering among the holm oaks and, in spring, in fields of yellow marguerite daisies and purple viper's-bugloss. Part of this area has been classified as a site of international importance.

V

English cheese from the Ambassador

FERIA HAD BEEN absent from Zafra for at least seven years and now had to turn his attention to the management of the family estates, while visiting and inspecting all the pueblos for which he was responsible.* For the next few years he spent little time at court in Madrid (Philip had moved the capital there in 1561) and was not officially involved in advising his king on relations with England and France. But this did not stop him railing against Elizabeth in letters to Alvaro de Quadra, Philip's ambassador in London, when the opportunity arose.

When Chaloner arrived to take up his post as ambassador in Madrid in the spring of 1562, he was not a happy man. The overland journey in mid-winter had been cold and uncomfortable; despite his protests, his chests of books and clothes had been opened and searched by inquisitive inquisitors; and he had only 'one sorry chamber for my lodging' until his predecessor, Sir Thomas Chamberlain, had left. He never liked Madrid: apart from the interference of the Inquisition and the cost of living, he could not stand the climate. 'This air of Madrid is subject to sudden heats... and straight again to sudden cold, as a man shall not know how to govern himself.' Chaloner was something of a hypochondriac: he complained of 'quartan agues' (regular bouts of fever) which he attributed to the weather, involving many sleepless nights during which he would compose and translate Latin verses.

It was fortunate, and somewhat surprising in view of his dealings with Feria in Flanders, that he found a sympathetic friend in Feria's wife Jane. They not only shared a dislike of the Spanish weather, but also of Spanish food. The weather they had to endure, but Chaloner knew a merchant in

---

* They included Feria, La Parra, La Morera, La Lapa, Alconera, Villalba de los Barros, Aceuchal, Santa Marta de los Barros, Nogales, Almendral and Corte de Peleas.

Bilbao who could help with the importing of produce from England. He
was an Englishman, John Cuerton who, having lived in northern Spain for
some years, was so well regarded by the Spanish authorities that he was made
a junior member of the bureaucracy of the Inquisition. Chaloner had stayed
with him on his way to Madrid, when they went hunting together for wild
boar. Cuerton became Chaloner's most important agent in Spain, supply-
ing him with information as well as food and clothing for the embassy and
for the Countess of Feria. Correspondence between Chaloner and Cuerton
confirms that, in June 1562, Cuerton was sending four cheeses from Bristol
and Shropshire to Madrid, two for Chaloner and two for Jane. In August of
the same year Cuerton sent 'a barrel of raisins of Corinth for the Countess of
Feria and 60 pairs of shoes'—also doublets, hose and shorts for the ambassador. Chaloner was asking Cuerton for butter, but it had apparently been
lost or stolen on the sea passage between Plymouth and Bilbao. Another
English agent, Hugh Tipton, resident in Seville, sent 'a barrel of salmon
and one of red herrings' to Chaloner and a similar quantity of fish to Jane.
The Ferias would spend part of the summer months in Madrid, where it
was slightly cooler than in Zafra, and presumably the various consignments
were collected from the embassy.

When another supply of English butter, intended for Jane and for
Chaloner in Madrid, was impounded at Bilbao in the autumn of 1562,
Cuerton was obliged to use his contacts and diplomatic skills on behalf of
Jane's good friend Susan Clarencius. An Englishwoman, together with a
younger man, arrived in Bilbao on their way to work as servants to Mrs
Clarencius, but were arrested by the port authorities, not for carrying two
firkins of butter but for having in their possession what was judged to be
a heretical book. The names of the Pope and St Thomas Becket had been
blotted out, possibly as many as 25 years ago after the promulgation of the
Act of Supremacy by Henry VIII. The likelihood is that the woman, to
whom the book belonged, had no idea it would cause trouble, and Cuerton
was able to persuade the authorities in Bilbao not to imprison her. However,
he told Chaloner of his irritation, not with the ignorant maidservant but
with Mrs Clarencius who seemed unconcerned and quite prepared to leave
the poor woman to take her chance with the Inquisition. She was also
reluctant to pay for the woman's keep while she remained in Bilbao, saying

that her maid should find another employer there, 'because she will be at no more charges with her'. Cuerton became more annoyed and told Chaloner that he didn't think much of Mrs Clarencius's honesty. After several weeks Chaloner and Cuerton were able to persuade the Archbishop of Seville to support the maid's cause, and he instructed the ministers of the Inquisition in Calahorra to release her. She and her companion were permitted to return to England, and Mrs Clarencius sent some money to the embassy to pay for the maid's expenses. When Mrs Clarencius left Madrid in the middle of October in company with the Ferias to spend the winter in Zafra, Chaloner reported their departure to Cecil. The ambassador and Mrs Clarencius may have temporarily fallen out over this episode, but the following year he was sending her his commendations 'a thousand times' in a letter to another of Jane's ladies, Mrs Damascene Stradling. Mrs Clarencius was now in her mid-50s, 'a good old woman' in Chaloner's words, and it is unlikely that she travelled to Madrid again. The Ferias' four-year-old son Lorenzo was taken ill during 1563 and she would have been in Zafra to look after him. One of Chaloner's associates, Robert Moffett, wrote that he was praying for 'that noble imp' and sent his commendations to Jane's 'gentlewomen'. Mrs Stradling wrote to Chaloner in September to tell him that 'Don Lorenzo has had a continual burning fever since August 10th, so extremely handled that it is to be marvelled how he lives. He hath not been let blood; my lady would in no wise consent thereto'. No further mention of Mrs Clarencius appears in the records after 1563, so it is presumed that she died in Zafra.

Chaloner had a difficult time during his four years in Madrid. English ships were attacking French vessels and relieving them of their cargoes—a practice to which Elizabeth's government turned a blind eye—but when Spanish shipping was intercepted as well, Philip reacted by ordering all English ships trading in Spanish waters to be seized and their crews imprisoned. It fell to Chaloner as ambassador to intercede on behalf of the English sailors, whom the Spanish authorities treated as pirates. Chaloner was able to secure the release of some, but many of them were incarcerated in extreme conditions in small ports and were never heard of again.

For a time, while Mary Stuart was queen of France as well as Scotland, Philip was in effect Elizabeth's protector. He was equally opposed to Mary claiming the English throne and handing power to the Guise family (her uncles were the Duke of Guise and the Cardinal of Lorraine, her mother Mary of Guise). But the situation changed after 1560 when Mary of Guise died, her daughter left France as a widow and Philip made a political marriage with Elizabeth of Valois. Elizabeth sent armed aid to the Huguenots, prompting Philip to threaten active support for the Catholic cause in France and its regent Catherine de Medici. Chaloner was told by Cecil to deny that any English troops had been sent to France, but was considerably embarrassed when their presence on French soil was independently confirmed.

Chaloner had other worries: the sinister presence of the Inquisition threatened not only foreigners resident or travelling in Spain but the ambassador himself. In 16th-century Spain there was no law of extra-territoriality or convention of diplomatic immunity to allow, for instance, an ambassador to eat meat on Fridays and during Lent. Nor was the English ambassador in Madrid permitted to hold Protestant services in his embassy because, according to the authorities, it might encourage the spread of heresy. The Spanish ambassador in London was permitted to celebrate Mass during Elizabeth's reign, although occasional raids on the embassy were made in order to arrest and prosecute any recusant Catholics found attending Mass there. Durham House became known, in Elizabeth's reign, as 'a trysting place for treason'.

While obliged to suffer these restrictions in his embassy, Chaloner's health was poor and he didn't have a wife to support him. But he had two consolations: the writing of poetry and translating of Latin verse, and his friendship with the Countess of Feria. No sooner had he arrived in Madrid than he and Jane were sharing consignments of food from England via John Cuerton's agency in Bilbao. Both Feria and Jane are complimented for their 'frankness' towards the English in Spain—the word in its 16th-century meaning would embrace hospitality and generosity—and Chaloner was no doubt grateful to them for making his time in Spain less disagreeable. In 1563 Chaloner was writing to Jane that the 'broils' in France required his presence in Madrid, but that he hoped to visit her in Zafra in the near future. 'Your honour may esteem that both of you are my avowed Spanish saints,' Chaloner wrote, 'whom I will in my stations make my first devotions unto.' He did not forget to ask after Jane's three-year-old son, hoping that 'Don Lorenzo may love a grammar as well as his father loves a gavillan'.*

* Gavilán is the Spanish word for a sparrowhawk.

The King's proposed trip to Monzón (where meetings of the Cortes of the crown of Aragon were held) might give Chaloner the opportunity to escape to Seville and on his way to stop at Zafra and kiss her hand. Jane wrote to say she was sorry that 'in this busy time of trouble she cannot harbour him in this simple lodge'. She may have been referring to her second son, Pedro, who was born around this time and lived only three months. Chaloner never did get to Andalusia, writing rather pathetically to Jane in 1564, 'I am now a confirmed invalid and cannot visit you at Zafra'. He was still working on behalf of the English sailors in prison; of those who had not died of disease or maltreatment, most were eventually released thanks to Chaloner. He wrote a number of letters begging to be recalled to England, and pointing out that 'I have never had one letter of thanks from the Queen'. He also invited the Ferias to stay with him at his estate at Steeple Claydon in Buckinghamshire. It was April 1565 when he finally embarked for home from San Sebastian and died six months later, having married for a second time. Cecil was chief mourner at his funeral in St Paul's Cathedral.

Chaloner's successor in Madrid was not a success. An academic scholar and dean of Gloucester, Dr John Man was in his mid-50s when he arrived in Madrid in 1566. (The year following Chaloner's departure was covered by William Phayre as chargé d'affaires, who a few years later was imprisoned in the Tower and executed for treason.) Man has been described by a 20th-century historian, Garrett Mattingly, as 'among English ambassadors perhaps the outstanding example of the emissary of bad-will... Just why Elizabeth and Cecil thought that a bigoted Protestant divine, without tact or breeding, would prove a successful representative at that ticklish point in Anglo-Spanish relations is a mystery.' Man may not have been all bad—he was on good terms with Philip's wife, Elizabeth de Valois—but he was heard to speak irreverently of the Pope, calling him 'a canting little monk', and he upset the Count of Feria over his comments about Jane's English relations. He also reported to Cecil that he had heard Jane saying how she 'marvelled how God could prosper the realm, seeing that they were all heretics and lived worse than Turks and Jews'. This was foolishly and seriously undiplomatic: the Ferias were not only accepted as patrons of the English community in Spain, but they were both invariably consulted by Philip on issues relating to policy towards England. An Englishman in Madrid wrote that Man 'doth dishonour the Queen and shame the country. There is no ambassador in so little estimation as he is since he misbehaved himself unto the Count de Feria who always was a faithful friend to all Englishmen... Man is taken to be meeter to sow sedition than to maintain amity, he is of so simple a judgment and small understanding.'

Man accused Feria, and also Jane's relatives, of open hostility towards him, and Feria accused Man of being 'pernicious and evil-minded'. He was accused of proselytising by the Inquisition, forbidden to hold Protestant religious services at the embassy, then banned from court and ordered to live in the village of Barajas outside the city. Elizabeth took this as an insult demanding Man's recall to London in 1568. Philip instructed his ambassador in London to explain to Elizabeth that it was only Man's behaviour that had necessitated his expulsion. The Ferias, he said, should not be held responsible for what had happened, nor should Jane's relatives be blamed; but Elizabeth appointed no more resident ambassadors to Madrid. The Spanish invasion of England was only two decades away.

Barely 30 years old, Jane was not only the doyenne of English Catholics in Spain but, with the exception of the egregious ambassador Man, she made a point of keeping in with Elizabeth's representatives in Spain. She had also been on good terms with Chaloner's predecessor, Sir Thomas Chamberlain, who sent his commendations to her and the family from Bayonne, on his way home, and then from London, together with 'a rundlet [barrel] of raisans and corrants, which is my wife's token'. In one letter to Chaloner Jane showed great tact in writing that she was 'most joyful of the Queen's recovery' from smallpox, and Chaloner passed her sentiments on to the Queen. Jane had many relations in England, at least two of whom were in Elizabeth's service, and she would not have wished to prejudice their careers by showing open hostility to the Queen. Jane's uncle, Sir Henry Sidney, was Lord Deputy of Ireland, and his wife Mary (née Dudley, sister of Robert) was Elizabeth's principal lady-in-waiting.

The Queen wrote to Jane in August 1568, partly in her own hand: 'To our right dear and right entirely beloved cousin the Duchess of Feria' (her husband had been made a duke the previous year)—

'Madame: Although such length of time and numbers of years are passed since we heard from you, considering our place and estate and your natural duty to the same, we might think you very forgetful thereof. Yet your cousin William Harrington bringing to us... [illegible] and certain good tokens of your well-meaning, which he also with the earnestness of your good will have at length offered to us, we could not but thankfully receive them, otherwise than before we were determined, having had an intention to have accounted you as a stranger and a forgetful subject, which meaning, upon the hope of your dutiful behaviour towards us, we are now content to change, and yet cannot, but by these few lines, express.'

After that long-winded sentence, Elizabeth referred again to Harrington, 'whom we do very well like', and passed on 'very hearty commendations to your husband the Duke of Feria'. She signed herself 'Your Sovereign and friend Elizabeth R'. Though no record of it remains, Jane would surely have sent a reply to such a letter from her queen who cannot have expected, and did not ask, Jane to return to England and renounce her loyalty to the Catholic faith. Elizabeth was also gracious enough to convey her good wishes to Jane's husband, who had never concealed his antipathy towards her, and whom she blamed for the state of Anglo-Spanish relations.

Jane played her hand cleverly during these years. While encouraging Philip to remain on friendly terms with Elizabeth—she had more trouble in urging her husband to do the same—she was doing her best to promote the English Catholic cause, whether through contacts with English exiles in Spain or correspondence with men and women of influence in England. One of these was Lady Margaret Douglas, Countess of Lennox, who was a niece of Henry VIII, half-sister of James V and mother of Lord Darnley who became Mary Queen of Scots' husband with encouragement from Margaret. Having been a lady-in-waiting to Elizabeth's mother Anne Boleyn and a bridesmaid at uncle Henry's sixth marriage, to Catherine Parr, Margaret won the confidence of Catherine of Aragon's daughter Mary, who favoured her to succeed to the throne on Mary's death. After all, she had been the lady of highest rank in England when the princesses Mary and Elizabeth were declared illegitimate. When her son was murdered, Margaret denounced his wife Mary, and this led to a temporary truce between Margaret and Elizabeth which lasted some four years until Margaret's husband Lord Lennox died and she was reconciled with her daughter-in-law. Margaret was in and out of the Tower of London for much of her life, for having incurred the displeasure first of Henry VIII and then of Elizabeth. One

Queen Elizabeth's letter to the Duchess of Feria.

of the charges against Margaret related to her secret correspondence with the Ferias, over the question of who should be the pretender to the throne: Margaret or Mary. When she died in poverty, Elizabeth met the costs of her burial in Westminster Abbey.

Having made Margaret's acquaintance at Mary Tudor's court, Jane was receiving letters from her almost as soon as she had settled in Spain, and Margaret's gentlewoman, Jane Baillie, wrote at least once to Susan Clarencius. This letter, and much of the correspondence between Margaret and Jane, were seized by the English authorities. Jane's letters to Mary Queen of Scots, however, often evaded Elizabeth's security network. Around this time a meeting was being proposed between the Scottish and English queens, but Elizabeth sent Sir Henry Sidney north to tell Mary it would not take place, ostensibly because of the civil war in France. In 1563 Elizabeth proposed that her favourite, Robert Dudley, should marry Mary, presumably so that she could keep both of them under her wing. But Dudley made it clear that he was not available for a Scottish match.

Dudley, son of the Duke of Northumberland and brother of Guildford, was something of a chancer. He was condemned to death by Mary but avoided his father's and brother's fate and went off to France with Mary's blessing to fight for the Habsburgs under Philip II against the French at the Battle of St Quentin. A few years later, when marriage was being rumoured between Dudley and Elizabeth, and he was intriguing against Cecil, Philip's ambassador apparently offered his help in getting rid of Cecil if Dudley would bring his queen back to the true faith. Another idea, discussed between Mary's Secretary of State, William Maitland of Lethington, and Spain's London ambassador, Alvaro de Quadra, was that Mary should marry Philip's son Carlos. But nothing came of it. Philip, indecisive as ever, prevaricated, and after waiting for almost two years, while Quadra and Lethington became ever more frustrated, Mary went off to marry Darnley. Elizabeth raised Dudley to the earldom of Leicester, and official contacts with Spain were discontinued.

VI

Two naval adventurers

UNOFFICIAL CONTACTS, however, showed no signs of slowing down and often involved English adventurers who maintained contact with both sides and were known to Jane. It was John Hawkins, a naval commander and sometime slave trader, who in 1571, having intercepted letters from Mary Queen of Scots to Philip and a Latin prayer book which she had sent to Jane, sent them on to Cecil, now Lord Burghley. However, in the same year he was also offering to take 15 ships of the privateer fleet into the service of the Spanish navy. Such double-dealing was not uncommon among Englishmen who travelled or had business in Europe during Elizabeth's reign and acted as mercenaries in the Catholic cause while continuing to profess loyalty to their queen.

An acquaintance of Hawkins, George Fitzwilliam, contacted the Ferias in Madrid—he may have previously met Jane in England—and obtained an interview with Philip, representing Hawkins as a faithful Catholic who was anxious to help remove Elizabeth from the throne. The Ferias entrusted Fitzwilliam with letters and presents to Mary Queen of Scots, and Feria said he could arrange for funds to be sent to Hawkins for the equipping of his ships against Elizabeth's Royal Navy. Philip demurred but said he might be more interested if Hawkins were to get a letter of recommendation from the Queen of Scots. Fitzwilliam travelled to Sheffield where he had an audience with Mary, who gave him letters to the Ferias and to Philip, which Fitzwilliam showed to Burghley before taking them on to Madrid.

Elizabeth's growing conviction that forces loyal to Mary were about to make war against her realm were strengthened later that year by the hatching and uncovering of the Ridolfi plot to assassinate her. Not only were the King, his ambassador in London, Guerau de Espes, and Feria implicated,

Sir John Hawkins in 1581, aged 44.

but also the Archbishop of Rossano, papal nuncio to Philip's court (who became Pope Urban VII for 12 days in 1590). However, while giving his support, Philip remained doubtful about helping to put a former French queen on the English throne to the principal advantage of France. Mary's devoted servant and principal adviser, John Leslie, Bishop of Ross, was also one of the Ridolfi plotters. He had been appointed her ambassador to Queen Elizabeth, and in the spring of 1571 he was doing his best to persuade the Duke of Alba to invade England from the Netherlands. Burghley was in no doubt of Leslie's involvement, his plea of privilege as an ambassador was

Portrait by Antonis Mor, listed perhaps incorrectly as 'Milora Dormer Inglesa, Duquesa de Feria'.

Jane, Duchess of Feria, by Alonso Sanchez Coello, c1563.

The widowed Duchess of Feria in the habit of a nun.

Lady wearing a Cross, by Antonis Mor, 1567. Probably Jane's cousin Margaret Harrington , for whom Jane rebuilt the Santa Marina church and convent.

Gomez Suárez de Figueroa y Cordoba, 3rd Duke of Feria, shown leading the Spanish army to relieve Constance. Detail from portrait by Vicente Carducho.

rejected and he was imprisoned in the Tower in October. Burghley wrote to him to ask about the correspondence which had been passing between Mary and Philip via Feria (until his death in September) and through the hands of Hawkins and Fitzwilliam. Burghley presumably already knew what had been going on, and Leslie confirmed the messages and the messengers, pointing inevitably to Mary's active role in the plot. (He also gave evidence of the plan for Mary to marry the Duke of Norfolk, which led to his execution.) Leslie was not exactly betraying his mistress, but he wobbled under interrogation, criticising her character and saying she should never have married. This was not enough to get him out of prison; however, when he was released in 1574, having sent a Latin oration to Elizabeth asking for his freedom, he continued in Mary's service.

Hawkins was able to learn details of the Ridolfi plot by ingratiating himself with Spain's ambassador in London, Guerau de Espes, then passing on the information to Burghley. At the same time he was offering his services to Spain in order to obtain the release of prisoners from his ships who had been held in the Indies for two years since his plundering of Spanish vessels off the Mexican coast. A month before he died, the Duke of Feria wrote to Hawkins as 'a friend and a good Englishman', promising to use his influence to have the prisoners freed. (Feria still believed that Hawkins, as a good Englishman, was intent on restoring Catholicism in England and putting Mary on the throne.) The prisoners, who had been shipped to Seville and held by the Inquisition, were set free, Philip gave Hawkins a pardon for having plundered his vessels in the Caribbean, a Spanish peerage and a letter of credit for the repair of the English privateers in order to fight for Spain. The Spanish ambassador wrote to his master over several months urging him to make use of Hawkins in the service of Spain and the Queen of Scots. 'The more I see of Hawkins,' de Espes wrote to the King in October 1571, 'and the closer I watch him, the more convinced I am of his faithfulness in your Majesty's interests.' But Philip, who was being characteristically hesitant, was not at all convinced, nor was the Duke of Alba, whom he consulted. Alba had already come across Hawkins, having seized some of his ships in retaliation for Hawkins's raiding and capturing of Spanish treasure. Sir Henry Cobham, who had accompanied Chaloner to Madrid when he was appointed ambassador, returned in 1571 to demand the release of the English ships and the removal of de Espes from his post as ambassador in London. Feria met him in the Escorial and assured him they could settle the matter 'as true Englishmen' (adopting the nationality of his wife), but he died three months later before anything had been settled. Cobham was also demanding the expulsion from Spain of English Catholic refugees, which did not endear him to Jane who had been on friendly terms with him in Chaloner's time. Philip was not going to accede to that, nor was he going to do business with a man of such doubtful loyalties as Hawkins. He was judged to be untrustworthy and contacts with him came to an end. Not long afterwards, Hawkins was traducing Feria's memory by claiming that the Duke had tried to persuade him to assist in the northern uprising in England.

Hawkins was praised for his help in foiling the Ridolfi plot, and when he was wounded in the Strand by a knife-wielding passer-by, Elizabeth sent her surgeon to attend him. She made him treasurer and comptroller of the navy, which gave him scope for enriching himself as well as improving ship construction. When the Spanish Armada invaded he captained the *Victory*, distinguished himself in the battle and was knighted. At his death in the Caribbean in 1595, while on an expedition with his fellow Devonian Sir Francis Drake, he was described as 'covetous in the last degree' and prone to 'malice with dissimulation'. But he had—probably—remained loyal to his queen.

His only son Richard was also a naval commander and adventurer. Having accompanied his uncle on an expedition to the West Indies at the age of 20, he served with Drake before commanding a ship against the Spanish Armada in 1588. He then bought a ship from his father and set off for South America, ostensibly on a voyage of geographical discovery and surveying. But he also did a bit of plundering of Spanish vessels on the way, off the coasts of Brazil and then Chile, having sailed through the Magellan straits. Off Ecuador he met more than his match and was forced to surrender to the Spanish authorities, who generously promised him and his crew safe-conduct out of the country. But he was imprisoned by the Inquisition in Lima for more than two years before being transported to jail in Seville and afterwards Madrid. When Jane came to hear of this, she petitioned the King for Hawkins' release, in spite of the fact that he had spent his career fighting the Spanish and plundering their property and that his father had been less than honest with the Ferias some 30 years earlier. But a promise of safe-conduct to Hawkins had been broken and, Jane argued, he was therefore being unjustly held in prison. While in Madrid Hawkins wrote to Burghley to complain that his stepmother was withholding a ransom bequeathed to him by his father. Whether this sum was paid to Spain, or whether Jane's intervention was successful, Hawkins was released in 1602, eight years after his arrest, and returned to England where he was knighted and made Mayor of Plymouth.

While Jane was willing to meet or deal with any Englishmen who were passing through or detained in Spain, she spent much of her time in communication with English Catholic refugees from Elizabethan England. Many of them settled in Louvain, where Jane's grandmother was living until her death in 1571. She was related to the mother of a member of Parliament in Mary's reign, George Chamberlain, who was briefly imprisoned in the Tower in 1562. He was questioned about his contacts with Catholics abroad, in particular with his kinswoman the Countess of Feria, and after his release Chamberlain travelled to Louvain not long before Lady Dormer died. He then went on to Madrid, where he was granted a pension and acted as the King's messenger to the Duke of Alba in the Netherlands, before settling in Ghent and helping English Jesuit priests to return to England. Among Louvain scholars, John Fowler, educated at Winchester and Oxford, was one of the first printers of devotional works in English which were circulated throughout the Netherlands, and in Spain, during the 1570s. Two of them, *A Briefe Fourme of Confession*, translated from Spanish, and Sir Thomas More's *Dialogue of Comfort against Tribulation*, were dedicated to 'the Ladie Jane, Duchesse of Feria', in recognition of the part she played in making Catholic literature available to English exiles.

There was one particular ally, Sir Francis Englefield, with whom Jane maintained close contact, in Flanders and Spain, for many years. Born in 1522, Englefield was knighted at the coronation of Edward VI but joined Mary's household before she became queen. She made him one of her privy councillors, also Master of the Court of Wards, and he shared her enthusiasm for persecuting heretics. Englefield and Jane Dormer became good friends during the Queen's reign, and years later his nephew would marry the daughter of Jane's half-sister Mary. When Queen Mary died, Feria noted that Englefield was 'a good man and a good Christian'; they both left England for the Low Countries during the same month of May 1559. While Englefield was based at Louvain, Elizabeth demanded his return to England, and when he refused his English estates and possessions were confiscated. Having failed to persuade the Queen to restore his estates, he travelled to Madrid in 1566 and asked Philip, whom he had known in England ten years earlier, if he would help. Philip instructed his ambassador to raise the matter with Elizabeth but she remained obdurate. Englefield was now running short of funds—he received no revenues from England—and in 1568 he began his employment with the Spanish court and was granted a pension by Philip. He spent the next few years at the court in Brussels, where he managed the distribution of pensions to other needy exiles in Flanders, and helped Jane's grandmother to distribute alms among the poor of Louvain.

It was during his time in Madrid that Englefield renewed his friendship with Jane. When he moved to Flanders he kept his ear close to the ground, writing long letters to her from Louvain, with news and gossip from that city and from England. In one dated April 1570, he refers to the number of new Catholics arriving in Flanders, refugees from the northern rising in England, who regarded the conservative Louvainists such as Englefield as 'too severe and scrupulous, calling us the Puritans of the Catholics'. Among these was Dr William Allen, who founded English colleges at Douai and Rome, and was made a cardinal. He was the spiritual leader of the exiled English Catholics, a brilliant polemicist and the exile most feared by Elizabeth.

Englefield had also maintained his contacts in England. He wrote to Jane of the doings and loyalties of various English peers, and those of the Spanish and French monarchs, towards Mary Queen of Scots, who was now in custody at Tutbury Castle in Staffordshire. But he was anxious that his comments should not fall into other hands. He cautioned Jane to 'take care of my letters; though there be no treason, yet there is more than I say to any other, or were meet to come to other's eyes. Our Lord has so provided me with languages that in any other tongue than my own they need not fear my pen nor my tongue.'

In this and another letter to Jane three weeks later, Englefield wrote of his 'pain of the lack of your letters [though] it does not become me to complain'. He also expressed concern at debts incurred by Anne Hungerford, Jane's sister, who intended to leave England for Louvain and join their grandmother, Lady Dormer. He appeared to be trying to protect Jane from her sister, writing that begging letters from Anne had arrived in Louvain 'to be sent to you, directed to Saffra... but we have not dreamed of any such thing'. Thanks to Jane, who petitioned Dudley, a licence was granted for her to travel abroad, and Anne did come to Louvain the following year, 1571, not long before Lady Dormer died. Sir Walter Hungerford, Anne's husband, was clearly something of a rogue.* According to Henry Clifford, he

> 'much blemished his person and worth by base covetousness and disordered sensual living. He did not entreat his lady as was due to his wife and a gentlewoman of her rank, whereupon she pretended to leave to go beyond seas to her grandmother, where she might have liberty of conscience and serve God freely.'

Before she came to Flanders, Anne had obtained a divorce from her husband, who spent three years in the Fleet prison. In Englefield's words to Jane, this was 'neither sufficient for her recompense nor for his punishment', though he omitted to mention that she had also had an adulterous affair which was revealed in open court. She left the country voluntarily, though penniless and not without a stain on her character. After the death of Lady Dormer, Anne became quite a friend of Philip's sister, the Duchess of Parma, and received a pension from the King. Clifford tells us that 'to gentlemen distressed and poor students, her liberality was marvellous, always compassionate, a great alms-giver'. However, she continued to lean on her sister for financial support during the 32 years that she remained in Louvain until her death in 1603. Englefield was going blind in the 1570s; and he told Jane he was feeling 'sick of my old disease, the stone'. But he would live for another 25 years.

As Feria had now been a duke for more than three years, Jane was hopeful that her husband would, after long and loyal service, be given some job promotion. When she asked him why others with fewer responsibilities were promoted above him, Feria told her that dishonourable preferment

---

* His father was beheaded with Thomas Cromwell at Tower Hill in 1540.

was common practice at Philip's court but that his honour was paramount. Henry Clifford used his imagination to record this conversation:

> FERIA: 'Would you that I take gifts and bribes, or that my honour remain in the point it doth, and should? For if I would accept presents and gifts, you must cause the back door to be opened to pass them out; for your house would quickly be so full as it would not contain them. But to this day my honour hath not been touched with bribes, and shall I now begin?'

> JANE: 'If it concern your honour, in God's name let it be; for to uphold your honour, I had rather be poor than give way to the least decay thereof.'

Feria's patience and incorruptibility were at last rewarded when the King offered him the governorship of Flanders in succession to Alba. Such a move would be a 'game-changer' for Jane, enabling her to resume personal contact with Englefield and other friends and to extend her influence among the large community of English Catholic exiles in the Low Countries, who were there in far greater numbers than in Spain. Both she and Feria were longing to get away from the stifling Spanish heat and the squalor of Madrid and go back to Flanders. When Philip's fourth wife Anna arrived in Madrid in 1570, one of her retinue thought the city 'the dirtiest and filthiest in Spain'. Ten years earlier Feria had written to Cardinal Granvelle to say that both he and his wife longed to return to Flanders, and that her health was suffering in Spain's climate. He was writing after his experience of the royal court at Toledo in the height of summer. However, allowing for his exaggeration, the Ferias were undoubtedly looking forward to returning to a cooler, cleaner northern Europe where he would be in charge and she would be close to family and nearer home. Feria urged Jane to tell her grandmother that they would soon be with her, but something held her back, possibly a premonition that the longed-for move to Flanders might not happen. In the event, old Lady Dormer—she was 84—died in Louvain in the first week of July. Just two months later and with little warning, Feria died on 8th September in Philip's palace, the royal monastery of El Escorial, under construction between Madrid and Avila. He was 48.

VII

Widowhood in Madrid

DURING THEIR years together in Spain, the Ferias struggled with the running of the estate in Extremadura. Feria was no longer in receipt of a regular salary from the King, and his royal duties were few, but they would travel every year to the court in Madrid. They may have been in debt, but it did not stop them sending the sum of 20,000 ducats to Mary, Queen of Scots when she escaped to England in 1568. Nor did they neglect the needs of the villages which formed part of the estate. In the same year the Ferias (he was now a duke) founded a Franciscan convent at Villalba de los Barros, dedicated to Nuestra Señora de Montevirgen.

The Ferias' journey from Mechlin to Extremadura in 1559-60 was said to have cost 50,000 ducats, which had been loaned from a Genoese bank. Not only was Philip notoriously slow in paying his courtiers' salaries, but Jane was known to have an extravagant husband, even if much of his spending was directed towards charitable causes. She did her best to help him manage his affairs, but some debts incurred while Feria was ambassador in London were still outstanding, and his finances did not improve much after he was granted the dukedom in 1567 (though Philip did give him a grant of 25,000 ducats—most of which went to Mary Queen of Scots—and an annual allowance of 5,000 ducats). The King demanded Feria's presence at court during most of the last four years of his life, when once again he enjoyed Philip's complete confidence. Together they detained and imprisoned Philip's son Carlos, and as Captain of the Guard Feria was responsible for him until his death. The circumstances of Carlos's arrest were related three 100 years later by a Hispanophile, Sir William Stirling Maxwell, who records that at midnight on 18th January 1568 Philip, plus a number of his trusted courtiers and 12 guards, proceeded to his son's apartments. The King wore armour under his dressing-gown and a helmet on his head, and Feria walked in front of him carrying a lighted candle. When they entered the apartment, Carlos's sword, dagger and pistol were seized from his bedside, and the windows of his rooms were nailed up. Philip told him, 'Henceforth I am going to treat you not as a father, but as a king', and Carlos, who was an invalid and mentally unstable, remained a prisoner until his death six months later. Philip's wife Elizabeth of Valois, to whom Carlos had been briefly engaged, died in October of the same year.

Feria was then sent on a diplomatic mission to Lisbon, and he was entrusted with dealing with Sir Henry Cobham when he came to Madrid to demand the recall of Spain's ambassador in London. As Captain of the Guard he was also kept busy organising parades and processions to greet Philip whenever he returned to Madrid from the half-built monastery/palace of El Escorial, or from his hunting lodge of El Pardo. During 1569 Feria's mother, Catalina, Marchioness of Priego, died and passed the title and the Priego estates to his younger brother Alfonso, who had married Feria's niece when he broke off the engagement, much to his mother's annoyance, and married Jane. Jane's relationship with her mother-in-law, understandably cool on the rare occasions that they met, had improved, in Henry Clifford's words, to one of 'mildness and affable respect'.

Once Feria had been appointed next Governor of the Netherlands, Philip was happy to give him responsibility for Anglo-Spanish trade negotiations relating to the Low Countries. The Duke of Alba thought the King, influenced by the Ferias, was too well disposed towards Elizabeth. This might have been true of Jane but her husband never changed his outspoken opinion of the English queen. In the last week of August 1571 Feria decided to make a will before he and Jane left Spain. He may also have been concerned for his health because, after a short illness, he died on 8th September and was buried in a monastery near the Toros de Guisando, where he and Jane had stopped in 1560 on their way to meet the King in Toledo. Clifford tells us that he bequeathed to Jane his soul, his son and his honour. He also left her debts of 300,000 ducats.

Jane was now a Spanish widow and, according to the custom of the country, would retire from public life and spend her time in pious contemplation and prayer. She always wore black, and in later years also wore the habit and scapular of the Third Order of St Francis.* A portrait of the widowed Jane hangs in Burton Constable Hall in Yorkshire.† She is wearing a black cloak over her nun's habit, and is carrying a prayer book with her index finger marking the place where she has been reading. She was only 33 when her husband died, but was not going to spend the rest of her life as a recluse at the Feria castle in Zafra. More financially responsible and with better judgment than the Duke, Jane was determined to pay off the family debts and leave her son a solvent estate when he attained his majority nine years hence. Shortly after Feria's death, tacitly acknowledging his responsibility for some of Feria's debts, Philip granted revenues to Lorenzo through the Order of Santiago.

She began by repaying debts incurred in London when Feria was ambassador and the bank loan taken out for their journey from Mechlin to Extremadura some 12 years earlier. Construction of the convent at Villalba de los Barros was halted and would be completed years later by her son. (The statue of the Virgin brings many pilgrims to the convent today.) The estate yielded an annual income of about 100,000 ducats, and with careful management all debts were in due course discharged. As Jane was now living in Madrid, she had to rely on managers and accountants in Extremadura who, under her instructions, administered this vast estate of more than 100,000 hectares, incorporating some 15 villages. However, Jane was considered to be a model, albeit absent, employer, whose tenants and estate workers, according to Henry Clifford's account, raised 26,000 ducats in 1603 to help her buy an adjoining estate near Badajoz for her son Lorenzo when he was Viceroy of Sicily.

Exiles from England, Ireland and Scotland who came to Spain could always expect a welcome from Jane if they found their way to Zafra or to her house in Madrid, and she would give food, clothes and money even to those who did not follow the Catholic faith. When any were imprisoned, such as Sir Richard Hawkins, who was an admiral in Elizabeth's service, she

---

* This was also worn by Catherine of Aragon in later life.

† Another version of this portrait belongs to a Dormer descendant at Chipping Campden in Gloucestershire. Also at Burton Constable is a portrait of Jane painted by Alonso Sanchez Coello in the early 1560s. There are three other versions of this portrait—at Rousham Park in Oxfordshire, Chipping Campden and the English College in Valladolid.

would use her influence with Philip in order to obtain their release. Seamen arrested and incarcerated in Seville also had reason to be grateful for her intervention.

Now that the position was open, a concerted move began, within a month of Feria's death, to have Jane appointed Governor of Flanders in his stead. Two letters from Antwerp, dated 6th October 1571—one addressed to Philip, the other to the new 12-year old Duke of Feria—were signed by 28 English Catholic exiles, among them doctors of divinity, licentiates, bachelors of theology and a Carthusian prior, Maurice Chauncy, who had accompanied Feria when he left England in 1559. The first signatory, and instigator of the letters, was William Allen, spiritual leader of the exiled Catholics in the Netherlands, a noted polemicist and the Englishman most feared by Elizabeth and her ministers. Lancashire-born and educated at Oxford University, when Allen refused to take the oath of supremacy he took refuge in Louvain in 1561. Having returned briefly to England because of ill health, under the protection of the Norfolk family, he went back to the Continent and there founded an English Catholic college at Douai, training and ordaining seminary priests to return to England to give spiritual comfort to Catholics living under Elizabeth. He helped to establish another college in Rome a few years later, and was made cardinal by Pope Sixtus V in 1587, the year before Philip's attempted invasion of England. It was then that Allen and his close ally, the Jesuit priest Robert Persons, made a serious misjudgement. They were convinced, and convinced Philip, that the Catholic faithful in England were all anxiously waiting for the Spanish fleet to invade and get rid of 'this woman, hated of God and man'. But Philip had already had a spell as king of England some 30 years earlier when married to Queen Mary. The majority of England's Catholics, while wishing fervently for their religion to be restored, would rather keep their queen than have the king of Spain back again. While Jane was at one with the beliefs and ambitions of Allen and Persons, she was careful to distance herself from too open an association with their objectives when the Armada invasion was being planned.

At the end of November 1571 Pope Pius had written a letter of sympathy to Jane on the death of her husband:

'Beloved daughter in Christ, noble lady, greeting... We took it sorely to heart, by reason as well of your personal loss, which in our fatherly tenderness towards you affects us not a little, as also of that loss which we too have sustained by the death of such a man, ay, and one so eminently endowed with virtue and religion... We doubt not that you have derived no little consolation from your pious meditations. And if there be any need of admonition on our part, we earnestly entreat you to be of good courage, and thereby establish yourself yet more in that virtue and that religion of which in other matters you have given such signal proof...

'For ourself be sure that for the love with which we cherish the memory of your most illustrious husband, whatever fatherly affection towards children most dear may prompt, we have in store, and ready to be conferred upon you and your son in unstinted measure.'

Jane would no doubt have derived comfort from his Holiness's words. At the same time her attention was directed towards Flanders and the governorship for which she was not lacking powerful support. She also needed papal approval, but Pius had only about three months to live, and was unlikely to have given much thought to Jane's future beyond hoping that she would continue with her 'pious meditations'.

Another letter to Philip came from Jane's friend Mary Queen of Scots, who stressed that Jane's appointment would be good for Spain's cause in the Low Countries, following the ruthless regime presided over by the Duke of Alba, who had been Governor for the past four years. Mary also mentioned the Flemish climate, which would suit Jane much better than Spain, and no doubt nursed the hope, if only in her dreams, that the two might meet again. (Pope Gregory XIII gave his support, a few years later, to a plot to marry Mary to John of Austria when he was Governor of the Netherlands.) Mary also instructed her secretary, Gilbert Curle, to write to the Pope (now Gregory XIII) in the spring of 1573, with a supporting letter from Allen. She would be greatly comforted by having Jane near her (if in a different country) and asked the Pope to use his influence to persuade Philip to send her to Flanders. 'To this end,' Henry Clifford tells us, 'did her Majesty write to his Holiness, commanding his ambassador to solicit it very seriously as a matter very convenient to his service and her solace.'

The Pope responded positively, instructing the Bishop of Padua, nuncio in Spain, to take up the matter with Philip. Whether or not the Bishop approached the King directly, he did write a fulsome reference:

'The Duchess of Feria is worthy of every favour and grace that the Pope has to bestow, both by reason of the merits of her late husband... and by her own devoutness... and because she has ever aided and supported all the poor English exiles for religion's sake, and that too beyond what her means may bear, nor does she ever fail to aid the cause, public and private, of the Catholics of that realm, besides which she is a most holy and religious lady... I knew this lady in England as the favourite bedchamber-woman of the holy Queen Mary... and she has ever since retained her purity of faith, nay, she has ever advanced in Christian piety and holiness of life.'

No doubt Philip agreed with all that, but he was anxious to have Jane around to offer him advice on Spain's strategy towards England following the discovery of the Ridolfi plot. After all, both Philip and Feria were implicated, the Spanish ambassador in London, Guerau de Espes, had been expelled and Philip was anxious not to antagonise Elizabeth any further. Whether for this reason, or because Alba persuaded him that Jane as Governor of the Netherlands would adopt too pacific an attitude to its people, Philip decided to keep Alba as Governor until 1573. Much as he admired Jane, Philip was not going to moderate his policy towards the Flemings, regardless of the fact that his father and his son had urged him to do so. Unlike Feria, who would willingly do his master's bidding, Philip feared for his uncompromising policy towards the Netherlands in the hands of an Englishwoman intent on reaching an accommodation with its people. After Alba, Philip appointed Luis de Requesens as Governor. His policy was more conciliatory than his predecessor's, though he continued a military campaign against the Dutch Protestant rebels.

Jane's value to Philip was as his intelligencer. After her husband's death Elizabeth's court was more inclined to look favourably on someone who, after all, was the niece of Sir Henry Sidney, Elizabeth's Lord Deputy in Ireland, and connected to the Dudley family through his wife Mary, who was lady-in-waiting to Elizabeth. Whether or not Jane was in receipt of confidences from England which she passed on to Philip, she was one of his principal sources of information on Elizabeth's attitudes and likely policy towards Spain and France. When, for the last time, a marriage proposal was put forward for Elizabeth in 1579—her prospective husband was to be the Duke of Anjou, half her age and brother of Philip's late wife—Jane was consulted by the English court. She may well have supported the renewal of an indirect link with Spain, but Elizabeth turned the young Frenchman down. Jane would also have picked up gossip from her network of English exiles, some of whom formed her household in Zafra and corresponded with relatives at home.

While Philip sought Jane's advice throughout the 1560s and 1570s, some of it, coming from the Vatican, did not always chime with the policy towards England which he was pursuing. Philip had twice blocked the excommunication of Elizabeth by the Holy See, and he was reluctant to take action to dethrone her for fear that she would be replaced by Mary Stuart who would further French rather than Spanish interests. But papal pressure, together with the influence of William Allen, began to push Philip towards war with Elizabeth. By now Jane was reluctantly accepting that she was unlikely to be making her future in the English Catholic centre of Louvain—where the refugee scholar John Fowler dedicated two of his recusant tracts to her. There was less reason to go once her grandmother had died, and she may have preferred not to live too close to her sister Anne Hungerford, who was now resident in Louvain and would have continually pestered her for money. So Jane stayed in Spain, ensuring that the Feria estates would be properly managed until her son was old enough to take on the responsibility. But she did not return to Zafra, preferring to be close to the seat of power in Madrid, where she also acted on occasion as lady-in-waiting to Anna of Austria, Philip's wife number four, who died in 1580.

Until the construction of the monastery/palace of El Escorial was completed in 1584, Philip spent much of his time at the palace of El Pardo, which he used as a hunting lodge, on the northern outskirts of Madrid. Here he established a portrait gallery, the majority of the paintings by Antonis Mor, court painter to the King, and Titian. Although most of them were lost in a fire in 1604, they had been catalogued and may have included portraits of Jane and of her cousin Margaret Harrington, painted by Mor. The historian and genealogist Argote de Molina, who published a detailed description of the gallery, calling it 'His Majesty's most majestic room', listed one portrait of 'Milora Dormer Inglesa, Duquesa de Feria' and another of 'Madama Margarita Inglesa'. Perhaps recalling his time in England, and the fact that both women had married Spanish courtiers, Philip may have commissioned

Mor to paint them, or asked their husbands to donate the paintings to his gallery. Perhaps Mor chose these two English ladies as representing the kind of feminine beauty—fair complexion and hair—to which Philip was known to be attracted. There is no doubt that two such ladies were painted by Mor in the early 1560s, and the portraits now belong to the Prado. But there is no certainty that they were originally hung in Philip's gallery and survived the fire, nor that they are portraits of Jane and Margaret Harrington. One of them, 'Woman with flower bracelet', was generally thought to be Jane, but doubts remain. The other, 'Woman with cross at the neck', may be Margaret Harrington but has never been positively identified. (Alonso Sanchez Coello, whose portraits of Jane are not disputed, was a pupil of Mor.)

While Feria was alive, and when he returned to court having been raised to a dukedom in 1567, he and Jane lived in a building known as La Casa de Oñate, off the Puerta del Sol. After Feria's death she moved to the district of La Latina, to a house described as *una casa noble*, facing the Plaza de la Cebada and next door to the church of San Andres. Madrid's principal grain market was held in this square, which in the next century became a popular site for public executions. Clearly Jane's lodgings were spacious and she lived in some comfort. However, the great majority of the city's inhabitants lived in single-storey whitewashed house made of brick and adobe. Madrid had a population of no more than 30,000 in the late 16th century, compared with about 80,000 for Toledo and Seville, and 50,000 for Valladolid. Philip may have moved the country's capital to Madrid in 1561, but conditions in the city's streets remained primitive for many years. There was no sewerage or street lighting; worse than that, the custom was to throw rubbish and human waste out of windows at night. The papal nuncio in Madrid in the 1590s, Camillo Borghese (he became Pope Paul V in 1605), reported with distaste that the houses 'have neither doorsteps nor closets; in consequence of which, all perform their necessities in chamber pots which they afterwards throw into the street, a thing which afterwards creates an insupportable odour'. Jane would surely not have ventured out of her house on foot, preferring a horse or a carriage to take her to the banks of the River Manzanares or to the royal palace nearby. (It was originally a fortress built by the Moors, and was known as the Alcázar until destroyed by fire and rebuilt as an Italian-designed palace in the 18th century.)

Another visitor wrote of 'ridiculous facades crowned with gutters which drenched water down on passers-by... Enormous grilles which obliged one to go along the stream then in the centre of the streets'. Jane's principal concern, however, would have been the weather, which in Madrid was described as *tres meses de invierno y nueve de infierno* (three months of winter and nine of hell). Of course she would have carried a fan, but her dress would not have kept her cool in summer. Whether or not in widow's weeds, Jane would be dressed in black, as other women generally were, with a veil over her face and a shawl around her head. For recreation, she would attend one of the open-air theatres in the city or the theatre within the royal palace.

Juan Carlos Rubio Masa, historian and author of *El Mecenazgo Artistico de la Casa Ducal de Feria*, goes so far as to say that Jane never returned to Zafra after her husband died. In which case she spent the next 40 years in Madrid without ever leaving the city except to attend the royal court at El Escorial or Philip's hunting lodge at El Pardo. One might have expected her to make occasional visits to supervise and check on the running of the estate; there were still ladies of her household living at Zafra. Rubio Masa states, however, that she conducted the business of the Feria estate from Madrid, in correspondence with estate managers and accountants. When she began to organise the restoration and reconstruction of the convent and church of Santa Marina, which was dedicated to her cousin Margaret Harrington, she was in communication with the architect and builders, giving detailed instructions on how the rebuilding was to be carried out. Both her son and grandson visited Zafra during this time, and were able to check and oversee the work in progress.

The household at Zafra in the first years of the Ferias' arrival included Margaret Harrington, Anne Pickering, Eleanor Paston, two Stradling sisters, Susan Clarencius and two or three others. Mary's Catholic court was in effect transferred to Zafra, at least for the next decade. Susan Clarencius died in 1564, around the same time as Jane's second son died aged three months, and Damasyn Stradling in 1567. Jane wrote to tell Sir Thomas Stradling of his daughter's death, describing Damasyn as her 'daughter by election'—though the other sister, in a letter to her father, characterised the relationship rather differently. To Jane, she wrote, Damasyn was 'an eye, an ear, a tongue, a hand and all her breath and spirit almost'. What is clear is that the English ladies were there to bolster Jane's position at court, especially after her husband died. But it is uncertain how many remained at Zafra or followed Jane to Madrid.

After 1571 Jane became more closely involved in two causes which had been of great concern to her husband. The first was the question of pensions for exiled English Catholics, promised by the King but too often overlooked or unreasonably delayed. To Feria this was a matter of honour—something which was rarely recognised among Spanish courtiers—and Jane continued after his death to press for the honouring of these promised pensions.

The second was Feria's sponsorship of the Jesuits. The formation in 1539 of the Society of Jesus (Jesuits) by the Basque priest, Ignatius of Loyola, proved an inspiration to Feria for the rest of his life. His brother joined the Order, he was in touch with Jesuits such as Joseph Creswell while in England during Mary's reign, and it was largely due to Feria, together with one of Loyola's early disciples and first biographer, Pedro de Ribadeneyra, that the Order was established in the Netherlands. Born in Toledo to a noble Castilian family, Ribadeneyra attended the universities of Paris, Louvain and Padua, before working for the Society in Sicily. He reported to his master Ignatius in 1556, shortly before he died, that Feria was also optimistic about extending the Jesuit presence in England. Although Mary was not enthusiastic—she and Cardinal Pole turned down Feria's request at the beginning of 1558—he took Ribadeneyra to London with him in November to persuade her that opposition to the Order was misplaced. But it was too late: Mary's death put paid to the idea and Ribadeneyra went back to Flanders. He and Feria remained in touch, and after the Duke's death he settled in Madrid where he was in friendly contact with Jane for more than 30 years. Ribadeneyra dedicated two of his Lives of the Saints (*De Los Santos Extravagantes*) to Jane, and visited her during her last illness.

VIII

Uncertain loyalties

1571 WAS A significant year for Jane, and not only because her husband and grandmother died. Her father, Sir William Dormer, was re-elected to Parliament after about 25 years, and her half-brother Robert, who would become the 1st Lord Dormer, came to visit. While Sir William did not try to conceal his Catholic sympathies—he entertained the Spanish ambassador at Eythrope (where Jane was born) in 1566 and Catholic priests were occasionally given shelter there—Jane had written to Sir Francis Englefield in Louvain to ask him to warn her grandmother not to mention religion when writing to her son William. No doubt with Elizabeth's spymaster Walsingham in mind, Jane suspected that 'watch was being kept on their letters and people questioned'. In 1570 Englefield, as ever keeping his ear to the ground, warned Jane that her father's recusancy was slipping in old age. He was said to be 'beset by heretics....so that he breathes their spirit'. However, when Sir William's death in 1575 was reported to Philip, his ambassador wrote that 'he ended his days as a good Catholic'. His wife Dorothy went on to marry Sir William Pelham, Lord Justice of Ireland.

A plausible but untrustworthy soldier of fortune, Thomas Stukeley, entered Jane's life in 1571. Englefield had told her of him, and he was given a good reference by her uncle, Sir Henry Sidney, Lord Deputy of Ireland, who described Stukeley as a 'gallant captain' when he served under Sidney, and appointed him seneschal in Leinster and Wexford, where he acquired various estates. Having given loyal service to Queen Mary, and to the Habsburgs at the Battle of St Quentin, Stukeley had no difficulty in transferring his allegiance to Elizabeth, while pursuing a life of piracy. After a few years in Ireland, during which he made regular contact with the Spanish ambassador in London, he moved on to Spain in 1570. He was received at court by Feria and proposed to Philip an invasion of Ireland, which was opposed by Alba. But the King knew nothing of Stukeley's reputation—he had been described as 'a ruffian, a spendthrift and a notable vapourer'—and was sufficiently impressed by Stukeley's apparent return to the true faith to confer on him the knighthood of Calatrava. (Spanish courtiers also dubbed him the Duke of Ireland and he later styled himself Marquess of Leinster.) Jane was equally convinced of Stukeley's genuine conversion, or reversion, to the Catholic religion, having given good service to her uncle. She 'caressed and favoured' him, according to the papal nuncio to whom she wrote to plead his bona fides. However, his bona fides, his origins, his principles and his honesty were beginning to be doubted. (Some said he was a bastard son of Henry VIII.) Having failed to get Philip's approval for an invasion of Ireland, he decided to take his case to Paris, and when that was unsuccessful, to Rome. There he found favour with the Pope and with Don John of Austria, who gave him command of three galleys at the Battle of Lepanto. Two years later Stukeley met Don John in Naples and tried to persuade him to raise 3,000 men, with papal blessing, for a hare-brained scheme to sail to England and free Mary Queen of Scots from prison.

Communication between Stukeley and Jane continued: he supported her ambition to be governor of Flanders (the job went to Don John in 1576), he wrote to her from the Vatican, and he tried to involve her in Ireland, using her influence to have the Archbishop of Cashel dismissed. The Archbishop had written to Philip to tell him that Stukeley was not only dissipated, having squandered all his wife's money, but a rogue who had arrived in Spain by way of Portugal with a crew of Irishmen who believed he was sailing from Waterford to London. It was probably this that persuaded Jane that Stukeley was not to be trusted. At the papal court in 1577 he met James Fitzmaurice, a member of the ruling Geraldine dynasty in the Irish province of Munster, and together they persuaded the Vatican to underwrite the cost of 2,000 men and ships to invade Ireland. After a few days at sea Stukeley put his unseaworthy vessels into Lisbon where Sebastian, king of Portugal, induced him to change his plans. Stukeley failed to keep his rendezvous with Fitzmaurice and headed for Morocco, where he commanded Italian soldiers against the Moors and was killed in battle.

Jane made an error of judgment in giving her support to this dishonourable adventurer, but she inevitably came into contact with Englishmen in Spain whose character and motives were not always the purest, and there were plenty of unprincipled rogues around in the late 16th century. Jane's devotion to the Scottish queen and to her cause were such that she trusted a Welshman, Thomas Morgan, who spied for Mary over several years but whose allegiance was distinctly suspect. Born a Catholic, Morgan served two Calvinist bishops before being appointed secretary to Lord Shrewsbury, in whose house the Queen of Scots was detained. Morgan soon gained her confidence and she entrusted him with her correspondence. Shrewsbury's suspicions were aroused and Morgan was sent to the Tower. When he was released, possibly through the intervention of Walsingham's chief agent, with whom he was on friendly terms, Mary sent Morgan off to Paris to join her ambassador at the French court, Archbishop Beaton. It was around this time that Jane became aware of Morgan through letters which were sent to her by him from Mary. Jane was anxious to do anything which would help Mary, including using her influence with the English exiles to persuade them that Morgan was a man to be trusted. He was in effect ostracised by the Jesuits Allen and Persons, and suspected of dirty dealings in France. In 1583 he and a Dr Parry hatched a plot to assassinate Elizabeth, without Mary's knowledge. Elizabeth believed Mary to be implicated, and demanded that Morgan be extradited to London but the French king refused and sent him to the Bastille instead. While there he was visited by Gilbert Gifford, whom he enlisted in Mary's service as a messenger for her letters. Whether or not Gifford ever intended to assist Mary's cause, he was turned by Walsingham when he arrived in England. News of the Babington plot against Elizabeth—Morgan was one of those who recruited Babington—was gleaned from Mary's letters which Gifford passed to Walsingham. At Gifford's subsequent trial in Paris, he tried to implicate Morgan but Morgan refused to testify against him. The English ambassador in Paris described Gifford as 'the most notable double, treble villain that ever lived'.

While Morgan was in and out of prison in France, and consorting with a double agent, Mary continued to rely on him rather than Archbishop Beaton, her faithful ambassador in France. Her trust in Morgan continued until her death and she bequeathed him a diamond ring. Jane seems to have been similarly seduced by this unreliable Welshman, convinced that he was always acting in Mary's interests. While it is understandable, given the closeness of their relationship, albeit at a distance since their meeting at Amboise 25 years ago, that Jane wanted to do anything to support Mary during her imprisonment, her continuing contacts with Morgan after Mary's execution are less easy to explain, particularly as Allen and Persons refused to have dealings with him. Having been released from the Bastille in 1590, Morgan went to Flanders where the Duke of Parma prepared a case against him at the instigation of his English Jesuit enemies. One of them urged that Morgan should be sent to Spain to be tried by the Inquisition. Parma's advice to Philip was that Morgan 'attempts to sow cockle and intrigues and to undo everything that Cardinal Allen and Father Persons and other good Catholics are doing... both within and without the kingdom'. He was also accused of having betrayed many of Mary's followers while he was acting as her agent. He was jailed for three more years, at the end of which he was banished from the dominions of Spain.

So he went to Rome, met the Pope and began writing both to Jane and to her sister Anne Hungerford, urging that the time had come for the Duchess of Feria to move to Brussels. Cardinal Allen was in poor health and had only a few months to live. Jane was clearly tempted, but she needed no encouragement from her sister, with whom she had had a strained relationship, nor from a man of whose dubious character and past history she must have been well aware. To the unanswered question—why did Jane trust Morgan?—must be added another: why was Morgan so anxious that Jane should go to Brussels? Could he have hoped and expected that Jane, grateful for his assistance in her taking up residence in Flanders, might disclose to him information about the Catholic exiles which Lord Burghley (Walsingham had died in 1590) would be glad to receive? In any event correspondence between Morgan and Jane continued until after Elizabeth's death, for some time after her son Lorenzo, who suspected Morgan of treasonable activity, had convinced her that she should not leave Spain. Once James succeeded to the English throne, Morgan had the cheek to write to him, putting forward Jane's half-brother Robert Dormer as a candidate for an earldom, in view of all that she had done for the King's mother Mary and 'the service that she and hers may do you hereafter'. Morgan described Jane's son as 'a great personage' and brazenly told James that the friendship of the Duchess was important to the crown 'for the house of Feria will be a strong house in Spain'. He went on to give the King the names of two men who would serve him well in the Court of Rome. He also took it upon himself to warn the King that Sir Walter Raleigh had been plotting against him, while recommending that Raleigh's wife should be treated with compassion, since she was the daughter of Sir Nicholas Throckmorton who, while Elizabeth's ambassador in France, had done Mary 'very grateful service'. It was no surprise that James did not bother to answer a letter of such breathtaking impertinence. Morgan continued his intrigues in Paris, was accused of conspiracy by the French king and jailed for a further two years (his fourth term of imprisonment). He died about 1606, the year of Guy Fawkes's trial for the Gunpowder Plot, when Fawkes told the court that Morgan had proposed 'the very same thing in Queen Elizabeth's time'.

Jane's most steadfast friend was Sir Francis Englefield, who wrote frequently to her from Flanders and Rome on the prospects for an expedition, and an English uprising, to free the imprisoned Mary Queen of Scots. He was hopeful that the enterprise would be led by Don John of Austria, who was appointed Governor of the Netherlands in 1576. But Don John was not willing to divert his forces from Flanders, and he died two years later. Englefield made his way to Madrid, where he met up with Jane again, and together they worked to obtain pensions for English refugees coming to Spain. There were always fewer than in Flanders, but the numbers in Spain were increasing. For the next two decades all petitions were presented by Englefield, with recommendations, to a committee which would sometimes judge the applicants to be *bulliciosos* (troublesome)—meaning that their devotion to the Catholic cause was open to question. They were either transferred to another part of Spain's European empire—the young Duke of Feria suggested Sicily—or deemed not worthy of more than a small allowance.

Like Jane, Englefield was still concerned for the future of Mary Stuart, but by the early 1580s Philip was more concerned about France. When the Throckmorton Plot was discovered in 1584, Englefield's name figured prominently. At Francis Throckmorton's trial correspondence was disclosed between him and Englefield over the prospect of military action

which Philip was being urged to take against England. Throckmorton—
Nicholas Throckmorton, Elizabeth's former ambassador to France, was his
uncle—was executed for high treason and Englefield's English estates were
confiscated.

One man to whom Englefield gave his support over a number of years was
Nicholas Sanders, who left England in the same year as the Ferias and went
to Rome, where he was ordained. He attended the Council of Trent and for
the next few years was professor of theology at the University of Louvain.
Having published his strongly ultramontane tract, *De Visibili Monarchia
Ecclesiae* in 1571, which aroused great hostility in England and led to the
arrest, and worse, of any priests found in possession of it, Sanders went
back to Rome. He was a staunch supporter of Mary, and Englefield was
one of several exiles who urged both Philip and Pope Gregory that Sanders
should be made cardinal. He went to Madrid and was received by Philip,
who awarded him a pension, but Sanders could not persuade him to invade
England. Frustrated at Philip's indecision, Sanders wrote to Dr William
Allen, beseeching him 'to take hold of the Pope, for the King is as fearful of
war as a child of fire, and all his endeavour is to avoid such occasions'.

When the papal expedition to Ireland organised by Thomas Stukeley
and James Fitzmaurice got no further than Lisbon, Sanders was commissioned by the Pope to go as his nuncio to Ireland and incite the chiefs to
rise against the English government. There was even an idea that the Pope's
nephew would be installed as King of Ireland. Sanders was accompanied
by Fitzmaurice, a small papal force and a motley contingent of Spaniards.
Philip was careful not to give his formal approval to the expedition, as he
was still reluctant to open a breach with Elizabeth. In 1579 Sanders landed
on the coast of Kerry and raised the papal standard at Smerwick, persuad-
ing himself that the Lord Deputy of Ireland, Sir Henry Sidney, was a crypto-Catholic. But there was no general rising: Sanders had the backing of the
Earl of Desmond, and Philip sent reinforcements, but the expedition was a
failure. The invasion force at Smerwick was besieged and massacred by the
English, and Fitzmaurice was killed. Sanders took to the hills as a fugitive
and avoided capture for nearly two years. But in 1581 he died, probably from
cold and starvation. He never got his cardinal's hat, but he had the lasting
respect of the English exiles, one of whom wrote: 'Our Sanders is more

to us than the whole of Ireland.' His many controversial manuscripts on the English Reformation continued to circulate in Europe; in England he became known as Dr Slanders.

Jane was well aware of what was going on in Ireland, and having forwarded to the Pope two valuable religious images which had been taken from St Paul's Cathedral and passed through her hands, she was indirectly assisting with funding for the Vatican. She had been in contact with Msgr Sega, papal legate in Spain, in April 1578 to warn him that, since no news had been received of the expedition undertaken by Stukeley and Fitzmaurice earlier that year, it may have been aborted. Sega wrote to Cardinal Galli of Como to tell him he had no news of Stukeley or Fitzmaurice, but that the Duchess of Feria should soon have more information. 'She, as you should know, is an English lady of very high rank, and a holy woman who has the liberation of that country much at heart; besides which the Viceroy of Ireland is her uncle, so that it is likely that she has good intelligence from those parts.'

Sega was being naïve if he thought that Jane's uncle, Sir Henry Sidney, who had been Lord Deputy of Ireland, with two breaks, since 1565, was going to confide in his Catholic niece in Spain. However, they were on good terms: he had given his consent, albeit reluctantly, to Jane's marriage, and he had come to say goodbye to her at Dover when she left England in 1559. In 1576 Jane had written to her uncle with a reference for the Bishop of Emly, in Tipperary, who was passing through Madrid on his way back to Ireland. According to Jane, the bishop always 'speaketh great honour of you, of your bounty, piety and clemency', and she was asking the Lord Deputy to 'vouchsafe him your lawful and favourable protection'. Religious differences did not preclude respect for family ties.

Sidney had not shown any clemency when he put down a rebellion by Fitzmaurice in 1573 and had 700 soldiers executed. He would have known of his subsequent activities in Rome and his intended return to Ireland, but Sidney was recalled to London in September 1578. However, as a member of the Privy Council he was able to use his influence in the ruthless suppression of the forces brought to Ireland by Sanders and Fitzmaurice and of the men of Munster, led by Desmond, who supported them. When a few Spanish survivors made it back to Spain, and Jane became aware of their plight, she did what she could to support them with money for food. If Jane was upset by the part played by her uncle Henry in putting down the Catholic rebellion, she would have been no less embarrassed to learn of the activities of Sir William Pelham, Chief Justice of Ireland, who had married Jane's stepmother Dorothy after her father died in 1575. Pelham was more soldier than judge, and in this capacity was largely responsible for the destruction of the Earl of Desmond's lands and the indiscriminate killing of the peasant population. Having ruled much of south-west Ireland for 300 years, the Desmond dynasty was effectively wiped out. Plague, famine and the English colonisation of Munster followed.

Philip had been told that 'He who would England win / With Ireland must begin'. But in the early 1580s Philip, respecting the objections of his military advisers, was not inclined to invade either country. He was not irredeemably hostile to Elizabeth, he was in two minds about Mary succeeding her and being under the influence of the Guises, and his priority was to put down the rebels in the north and retain control of the Netherlands. Caution and procrastination were, as ever, Philip's watchwords; more bellicose words were issuing from the Vatican, but since the accession of Sixtus V in 1585, there was less enthusiasm for risking papal funds on an invasion of England. William Allen and Robert Persons were hatching plots against Elizabeth from Rome, news of which Jane passed on to Philip in Madrid. This irritated and embarrassed him and he ordered her to keep the Jesuits at arm's length.

In 1586 Mary wrote to Philip's ambassador granting her 'rights' to the English throne to Philip if her son James had not become a Catholic by the date of her death. The Babington plot (which Philip supported) was about to be exposed and, after years of isolation, Mary, by her own admission, no longer understood 'what line to sail, nor how to lift anchor'. At the same time Philip's closest advisers, including his half-sister Margaret of Parma, were dying and, due to repeated attacks of gout, he was in poor health for the next two years. After Mary had been executed, Catholics in England feared that a Spanish invasion would mean a Spanish infanta on the throne in place of Elizabeth, and most of them decided they preferred the English devil they knew.

Allen and Persons continued to rail against Elizabeth from the safety of Rome, where they completely misjudged the mood in England. Persons was involved in a plot to bring the Duke of Guise, Mary's first cousin,* to England at the head of an army several thousand strong, and after her death he was again urging Philip to invade England, declaring that all English Catholics 'without a single exception regarded the invasion with approval'. It is said of Persons, in the *Dictionary of National Biography*, that 'for nearly 20 years he was one of the most zealous promoters of the Spanish invasion of England'. Having joined the Society of Jesus in Rome in1575, he accompanied Edmund Campion to England and set up a printing press in Essex. When Campion was arrested and subsequently hanged, drawn and quartered, Persons escaped across the Channel and made his way back to Rome, remaining there until after the Spanish Armada invasion. Thanks largely to Persons, Allen was made cardinal in 1587, a promotion which encouraged him to launch a personal attack on Elizabeth. In his *Admonition to the Nobility and People of England and Ireland*, Allen denounced this 'incestuous bastard, begotten and born in sin of an infamous courtesan... this woman hated of God and man'. This was going much too far: while wishing for their religion to be restored, most Catholics in England had had enough of Philip as their king in the 1550s and they remained 'faithfullest true English subjects'.

The Irish, on the other hand, would have preferred a Catholic Spaniard to an English Protestant queen, But Philip forgot or ignored the old adage and decided not to begin with Ireland. Whether or not his deteriorating health throughout 1587 affected his capacity for rational decision, he seemed to have convinced himself, or been convinced by his ministers and naval officers, in line with Allen and Persons, that England's Catholics would fall at Spain's feet. On the contrary, many had been alienated by the failure of Spain to make overtures to them or to spell out what would happen in the event of a successful invasion. What finally decided Philip in favour of invasion was probably Drake's raids against the Spanish fleet, on both sides of the Atlantic. So the Armada sailed from Lisbon in May 1588, with a second-choice commander and misgivings expressed by both the Duke of Alba

---

*   He was the son of the Duke of Guise who took Calais in 1558 and whom the Ferias met on their way to Spain when they stayed with Mary Stuart, then Queen of France. Both Dukes were assassinated.

and the Duke of Parma. Elizabeth appointed her Lord High Admiral, Lord Howard of Effingham, from a Catholic family, to command the English fleet.

Following the failure of the Armada, Persons was still urging Philip to make another attack, but he had come to accept that no invasion could be successful while Spain had done nothing to encourage the support of Catholics in England. 'To think to get the upper hand in England,' he wrote to Philip's secretary and state councillor, Juan de Idiaquez, 'without having a party within the realm is a great illusion, and to think to have this party without forming it and keeping it together is a great illusion.' Elizabeth issued a proclamation in 1591 denouncing any plans for another invasion and mentioning Persons by name. He responded with a stream of invective against the Queen and her councillors which, when published, did nothing to assist the Catholic cause in England. At the same time he persuaded two English priests, whom he met in Valladolid, to 'undertake to kill her Majesty, and they took the sacrament to perform the same'. Having arrived in Spain they were imprisoned in the galleys at Ferrol in Galicia. News of their plight reached Jane, who used her influence to have them released, though without knowing of Persons' plans for them. However, both Englefield and de Idiaquez were privy to the plot. One of the priests died and the other, Gilbert Laton, was sent back to England with the almost impossible mission to intercept the Queen's carriage as she travelled between her palaces and attack her 'with a poignard'. Needless to say, the assassination attempt failed, and the unfortunate Laton, having confessed that he was acting on the orders of Persons and Englefield, was executed.

A couple of years later, Persons published a tract, under a pseudonym, entitled 'A Conference about the next Succession to the Crown of England' which argued the case for Philip's eldest daughter, the Infanta Isabel Clara Eugenia, to succeed to the English throne. Its inflammatory content, supporting the use of violence to remove a heretical ruler, caused further indignation among Catholics in England, while Parliament declared that anyone found with a copy in his house would be guilty of treason.

Jane was not going to associate herself with the immoderate language used by Persons and Allen (he died in 1594), but she was looking ahead to the succession after Elizabeth's death, though not her assassination. As

Philip's representative, the Duke of Feria (Jane's son Lorenzo) had already proposed to the States-General in Paris in 1593 that Isabel should succeed to the throne of France. However, in 1596 Jane and Englefield, together with several exiled English clergy, addressed a petition to Philip, with a lengthy accompanying document, giving 'Reasons why the English Catholics desire that the Infanta of Spain should succeed' to the English throne—principally because she 'descends directly through various lines of the royal house of England, and has more than one claim to the throne'. (Her mother was Elizabeth of Valois and through the house of Lancaster she was a direct descendant of John of Gaunt.) The document warned Philip that 'all hope of remedy will disappear' unless he 'takes this matter in hand... by giving orders that his Holiness should be energetically approached on the subject... It is meet that promptness should be used, as negotiations are going on to impede this object and to forward the succession of a heretic, which would be the total destruction of the realm and as a consequence of all the northern countries of which the conversion depends on that of England. This will be a divine work of piety and godliness on the part of your Catholic Majesty.' Jane and the other signatories to the petition tried their best, but it was not to be: Philip's gout was getting worse and his life was almost at an end. In the year, 1598, that he died he handed over sovereignty of the Netherlands jointly to his daughter Isabel and Archduke Albert of Austria, whom she married at the age of 33.

Englefield had been blind for several years and he died shortly after the joint petition had been sent to Philip. However, Jane had kept in regular touch with him; one letter survives which she wrote to 'Good Sir Francis' from Madrid in July 1593. It is a chatty letter, of no political or religious significance, but her brief mentions of Allen, Persons and Creswell* indicate that she was still in friendly communication with them. She goes on to tell Englefield that her cousin Margaret Harrington's daughter has had a fall 'so great and perilous. And her head hath been opened!... The physicians and surgeons say that it is now out of peril.' In a postscript Jane wrote, 'I dare say Father Creswell is no better fried in Seville than we be here since the

---

*   Joseph Creswell succeeded Persons as Rector of the English College in Rome and as head of the English Jesuit mission in Spain. He acted as chaplain to Englishmen serving with the Duke of Parma's forces at the time of the Armada.

caniculares* came in'. Englefield spent his last years at the English College in Valladolid and was buried there.

---

*   Derived from the Latin 'canicula' (little dog), she is referring to the dog days of summer, or the hottest period of the year.

IX

Perfumes and sweet waters

JANE WAS undoubtedly a supreme diplomat. While maintaining close relations with the principal English Jesuits—she met Henry Walpole shortly before he returned to England and to his martyrdom—and sharing their ambitions, she never openly declared her support for the Armada invasion, nor is there any surviving correspondence to confirm it. While Jane supported Mary Stuart's claim to the English throne, it was not her wish that Elizabeth should be dethroned, and there is no evidence that she was associated with any conspiracy to assassinate Elizabeth (though her husband did put his name to the Ridolfi plot). Jane was concerned not to embarrass members of her family in England and put their careers, and even their lives, in jeopardy. Sir Henry Sidney was a trusted adviser to Elizabeth and his wife Mary was for many years one of her favourite ladies-in-waiting. Their son Philip (the poet) married Walsingham's daughter and was appointed Governor of Flushing in 1585. Sidney and his wife, plus Philip and his wife all died in 1586, but Jane did not take the view that this gave her the freedom to express open hostility to Elizabeth. By now Mary had less than a year to live, she was fatally implicated in the Babington plot, and Jane must have realised that she would never hear from her friend again. She suffered some embarrassment when, in 1589, an unreliable Irish priest called Nicholas Sedgrave, a former associate of Thomas Stukeley, had the bizarre idea of negotiating with Robert Sidney, who had succeeded his brother Philip as Governor of Flushing, for the surrender of the town. Sedgrave approached the Duke of Parma, who had given him an army chaplaincy, to tell him that Sidney was 'an uncle of the Duchess of Feria, and he is not as heretical, or as pleased with the Queen's role, as may appear'. Parma encouraged Sedgrave to contact Sidney and went so far as to report his information to Philip. However, Sedgrave had got it all wrong: Jane and Sidney were first cousins but had never met, Sedgrave had never met either of them, and Sidney was a loyal subject of his queen. Jane was probably unaware at the time of the Irishman's clumsy intrigue, but a few years later Sidney declined the opportunity to meet her son in Brussels.

Among Jane's relations on her father's side, her half-brother Robert Dormer was a respected figure in Buckinghamshire, where he had inherited a large estate from their father. He was Sheriff of the county, Member of Parliament and knighted. His father-in-law, Viscount Montagu, had served Mary Tudor during her marriage to Philip, and continued his Catholic associations, but he was appointed as one of the peers who tried Mary Queen of Scots. Continuing their recusancy, Robert and his wife were never punished for hearing Mass, nor for having received the sacraments from Edmund Campion shortly before his arrest and execution.

Jane also had six half-sisters, three of whom did not marry. Margaret married into a prosperous Yorkshire family and lived at Burton Constable Hall,* north of Hull. Her husband, Sir Henry Constable, was a pillar of the county—Justice of the Peace, Sheriff, Member of Parliament for Hedon, which was surrounded by his estates—but he was often embarrassed by his wife's unbending devotion to the Catholic faith which, together with her connection to Jane, placed him under suspicion for several years. The Archbishop of York declared Margaret to be 'a most obstinate recusant and will not be reformed by any persuasion, or yet by coercion'. She and Jane probably never met—Margaret was born only six years before Jane left England—but it is appropriate that there are two portraits of Jane hanging at Burton Constable today.

Margaret refused to attend Anglican services and she harboured Catholic priests, one of whom confessed to saying Mass in the house. She was often arrested for recusancy and occasionally imprisoned. On one occasion, while detained in a Yorkshire jail with her friend Lady Babthorpe, they succeeded in bending back the bars of their cell window to receive the sacraments from a sympathetic priest. Before she was prosecuted for allowing Catholic priests to stay at Burton Constable, she was summoned before the Earl of

---

* The red-brick hall dates from the 1560s and incorporates the remains of an earlier manor house.

Huntingdon, who recommended leniency, possibly because of a tenuous link between his wife Katherine's sister and Margaret's father William Dormer via his first wife. When Margaret's husband petitioned the Queen, and agreed to guarantee her future behaviour, the case was dropped. But she remained an unrepentant Catholic, and after Constable's death an indenture was drawn up to restrict Margaret's movements. She was granted a suite of rooms at Burton Constable and a small garden, also permission to 'walk at her pleasure' in the long gallery of the house. She outlived her husband by 30 years, refusing to conform until her death, when she left crucifixes to her children in her will.

Another of Jane's half-sisters, Catherine, embraced the reformed church. She married Lord St John of Bletso, who was keeper of Tutbury Castle in Staffordshire while Mary Queen of Scots was imprisoned there. Their daughter Anne married the son of Lord Howard of Effingham who commanded the English fleet against the Spanish Armada. Mother and daughter were both buried in Westminster Abbey. Catherine's effigy shows her reclining, with her right hand supporting her head and wearing a ruff, stomacher and full skirt. The third, and eldest, half-sister, Mary, married Viscount Montagu's son (both were called Anthony Browne) and after he died she had two other husbands.

The connection by marriage of two Dormers with the Montagu family provides an example of how, in Elizabethan England, Catholics could survive if they kept their heads down and did not challenge the new religious order. Although Viscount Montagu's second wife, Magdalen Dacre, had been a maid of honour at Mary's wedding to Philip, Elizabeth was happy to accept the Montagus' hospitality for several days at Cowdray House in Sussex. Magdalen's brother Francis was a rather more militant Catholic who, belonging to a wealthy Cumbrian family, took part in the northern rebellion of 1569 against Elizabeth, the year after Mary escaped from Scotland and arrived in England. Some 20 years later he was in Scotland at James VI's court, and from there he travelled to Rome and on to Spain where, having been arrested in San Sebastian as a spy, he obtained his release thanks to Jane and Sir Francis Englefield. Philip then granted Dacre a pension and made him a captain of musketeers. Recalling her friendship with Magdalen when they had both served Mary Tudor, Jane offered her brother hospitality in Madrid, where he began plotting his return, with the help of Spanish forces, to reclaim his properties in England. After a year both Jane and Englefield judged him to be too restless and unreliable to be allowed to stay in Spain, and Persons went so far as to accuse him of being 'a spy for England [who] would burn the King's fleet'. So Dacre was sent back to Rome, before returning to Scotland in 1597 and bothering Jane no more. But she was reminded once again of the risks involved in trying to help those whose loyalties were not always clear.

Neither Sir Francis Walsingham nor Lord Burghley (Sir William Cecil having been ennobled in 1571) was ever able to pin anything significant on her. While they would have known of Jane's friendship with Mary, and her contacts with Allen and Persons and other Catholic exiles, she never gave Elizabeth's spymasters clear evidence of treason. Nor did Elizabeth accuse Jane of sharing Feria's hostile and aggressive opinions of her monarch. Jane's unswerving allegiance to the Catholic faith did not stop her from forming friendships with two ambassadors in Madrid, Chamberlain and Chaloner, while her husband was alive, plus two others, Cornwallis and Digby, in the last decade of her life. Nor did it prevent her from acting on behalf of sailors loyal to Elizabeth (both English and Irish) when they were held in Spain— most notably Sir Richard Hawkins, who had commanded a ship against the Spanish Armada. On another occasion she secured the release of 38 English sailors who had been captured in the West Indies, imprisoned in Seville and sentenced to death. The Mayor of Barnstaple, a Mr Norris, attested to her successful interventions on behalf of English merchants who had fallen foul of Spanish laws.

It was through Jane's connection with the Dacre family that a fascinating document was brought to England towards the end of the 16th century and is now in the British Library. It is Jane's guide to household management and cookery—a sort of precursor to Mrs Beeton—which she put together and wrote for the benefit of her English Catholic friends, both in Spain and in England. This slim volume came into the possession of Anne Howard (née Dacre), Countess of Arundel, at some time in the 1580s, after she and her husband had converted to the Catholic faith. (Elizabeth punished Anne with a year under house arrest, but the Earl of Arundel, who tried to flee to France, was imprisoned in the Tower, where he died.) In view of Anne's

Funerary monument to Catherine, Lady St John of Bletso in Westminster Abbey.

literary aspirations—she wrote some poetry and a journal recording her experiences, her emotions and the daily life of her household—and the fact that an Arundel cousin had served the Marian monarchy with Jane, she was happy to distribute Jane's manuscript among the English Catholic network. Those former ladies-in-waiting who had followed Jane to Spain and were living in Zafra and Madrid were also in receipt of her advice and tips.

It is described as the Duchess of Feria's prescription for 'how to perfume gloves, to make perfumes and sweet waters with divers other sundry preservatives as be made in Spain and Portugal'. Jane lists various ways to dress gloves, to make the inside of gloves yellow and to make gloves red using Cordovan dye. Jane undoubtedly played a part in increasing the popularity among Englishwomen of the Spanish fashion for perfumed gloves, in particular red ones. Her instructions for making perfumes require using 'paste of amber', 'oil of amber', 'sweet bags of roses', 'a little water of a sweet smell'. For 'a perfume for a chamber' Jane recommends 'oil of roses and storax' (a resin from the bark of a liquidambar tree). She explains how to incorporate amber for making pomanders, and prescribes perfumes 'for the rheum'. *Espliego* (lavender) should be used for sweet water to sprinkle over clothes.

When she offers recipes for cakes and biscuits, Jane frequently uses Spanish words, which would have confused her readers in England. How many would have known that *alcorza* is icing sugar, *rosada* means frosted, *rosquillas* are ring-shaped cakes, rather like doughnuts, and *bizcocho* is a sponge cake? To make a *bizcocho* (or *biscocha*) Jane uses walnuts, almonds, cinnamon, flour, honey, sugar, butter, eggs, and she specifies exact quantities. She also gives detailed instructions for preserving oranges, gourds and quinces, and a recipe for quince jelly. When she comes to *marmolet* (marmalade), which the Spanish have never really understood, in spite of growing Seville oranges, Jane turns to a Portuguese recipe, using quinces, sugar and orange water. The sugar, she advises, should be added 'proportionally as the sweetness or tartness of the quinces requireth'.

As an anti-ageing treatment for the hands, Jane prescribes a paste made with blanched almonds and sugar, which will be the more effective under leather gloves. The hands should be washed with rain water and oil of Benjamin (used by those of Moorish origin in Spain). For the last pages of the book Jane reserves her most exotic preparation, 'to preserve the face and make it smooth'. Though difficult to follow, the instruction is to 'take a pair of pigeons and defeather them, then take Venus [Venice] turpentine, 3 fl over with new-laid eggs thoroughly beaten, pour and stir; when all things incorporated together, put in to the pigeons and so distill them in alembic of glass'.

Jane's thoughts returned to more serious matters when, shortly after the remnants of the Armada returned defeated to their Spanish ports, she met Robert Persons for the first time on his arrival in Spain. Having come from the English College in Rome, his next enterprise, which had Jane's enthusiastic support, was to establish similar colleges in Spain. His first was founded in Valladolid and named in honour of St Alban, the first English Christian martyr, who was decapitated in the 3rd century at the Roman settlement of Verulamium. The college received royal and papal seals of approval, and Philip paid a visit in 1592, the year that Persons founded another seminary, St Gregory's, in Seville. As part of their training, these student priests were required to take an oath that they would return to England to celebrate Mass for recusant Catholics. They would often make their way south to Seville, then onwards down the river Guadalquivir to Sanlucar de

Barrameda, where Persons had arranged for a meeting house and church used as a refuge by English merchants (known as the Brotherhood of St George) to be restored and converted into a hospice for the seminarians. He also founded a similar community in Madrid, and Jane would do what she could to ensure that the missionaries had enough money, clothes and provisions before they sailed back to England, sometimes via Lisbon and Ireland, and to probable martyrdom.

The training of these young Catholics to infiltrate alien (ie Protestant) territory and undermine its government, with the attendant risks of arrest, torture and execution, puts one in mind of the agents of Special Operations Executive who, three and a half centuries later, were dropped secretly into France for the purpose of subverting the occupying power. And their chances of survival were no better than the missionary priests', who also faced the risk of encountering Catholic double agents in Spain, employed by Walsingham or Burghley on Elizabeth's behalf. By the end of the century well over 100 priests had been executed at Tyburn.

While Elizabeth's spymasters were employing agents in England and on the continent of Europe to root out English Catholics intent on under-mining the Protestant regime, Spanish ambassadors in London were acting much like MI6 station chiefs, using agents and local informants to send reports to Madrid on the state of religion in England and on Elizabeth's military capabilities. One such was Bernardino de Mendoza who, when sus-pected of links with the Throckmorton plot, was expelled from his post. He then went to Paris and continued espionage activities with contacts among Catholic exiles and even with the English ambassador in Paris, Sir Edward Stafford, whom Mendoza bribed to pass on secrets to Spain. Stafford also gave misleading information to London on the Armada preparations.

A successful network of spies reporting to Philip was established around this time by an enterprising Welshman, Hugh Owen. After travelling in Europe, meeting exiled Catholics, becoming fluent in several languages and supporting the Ridolfi plot against Elizabeth in 1571, Owen went to Flanders and began to organise the smuggling of information from London to Madrid. He gained the trust of the Duke of Parma, Governor of the Netherlands, and may have had a hand in planning for the Armada inva-sion. In 1590 Owen went to Madrid, where Philip appointed him in effect as his spymaster and gave him a pension. Back in the Netherlands, Owen struck up a friendship with a Flemish publisher, Richard Versteghen, and together they received coded information from England, often from Jesuits such as Henry Garnet and John Gerard, which they passed on to Spain as *avisos* (reports) decrypted and translated by Owen. On occasion copies of Privy Council correspondence, and even letters from Burghley, found their way across the Channel. Messages were carried by friendly merchants and by students on their way to the English Colleges in Flanders and Spain, and Catholic texts were smuggled from Flanders back to England. Archduke Albert, when he became Governor of the Netherlands in 1596, was impressed by how much valuable information Owen was able to gather. He asked Philip to honour Owen's 'great and special services in the affairs of England', and the King obliged by raising a supplementary pension for him for life. When Owen was wrongly accused of involvement in the Gunpowder Plot and his extradition was demanded, the Archduke intervened to act as Owen's protector. However, Owen had no liking for James, whom he called 'this stinking king of ours'.

No correspondence between Owen and Jane has survived, but she would have known of his network and may have met him when he was briefly in Madrid. They had a mutual contact in the Countess of Arundel, who distributed Jane's folio of recipes in England; she also acted as informant for Owen and Versteghen, who sent her reports to Jane's Jesuit friends Allen and Persons, and she gave her protection to Catholic missionaries in England. Persons went on receiving Owen's *avisos* after 1597 when he handed over the rectorship of the Valladolid College to Joseph Creswell, and went to Rome as Rector of the English College for the remaining 12 years of his life. Owen joined him there in retirement from Flanders.

Englefield, blind and with his health deteriorating, retired to the College in Valladolid, where he died and was buried in the chapel. Jane was a benefactor of the College, which acquired one of the Coello portraits of her in 2008. It is the only English College still open in Spain, with about 50 trainee priests resident in Valladolid for one year. Its most treasured possession is a badly damaged image of the Virgin, with hands and arms severed and nose removed from the horribly disfigured face. Only the tiny feet, no more than stumps, of the infant Jesus remain on his mother's knee. The statue has been in this state since 1596, when it was picked up in the streets of Cadiz, one of many sacred images removed from churches and houses and desecrated by Anglo-Dutch troops under the command of Lord Howard of Effingham and the Earl of Essex. When the statue turned up in Madrid a year or so later, the priests of the English College in Valladolid asked for permission to look after it in their chapel. It was named *La Vulnerata* (The Wounded One) and entrusted to the care of Catholic Englishmen in Spain—a poignant reminder of the destruction of Cadiz by Protestant Englishmen in the service of Queen Elizabeth. The statue remains there today, taken out of the College once a year to join the Holy Week parades in the streets of the city. Lord Howard of Effingham was rewarded by Elizabeth on his return with the earldom of Nottingham. Nine years later he went to Valladolid for the ratification of the Anglo-Spanish peace treaty and visited the English College at the invitation of the Rector, Joseph Creswell. It is not recorded whether he was shown or told the history of *La Vulnerata*.

Creswell (known to the Spanish as Cresuelo) went from Rome to Spain in 1592 to help Persons with the early years of the Valladolid and Seville colleges and to take responsibility for maintaining and keeping them solvent. The subsidy from Philip was continued by his son, Philip III, who visited the college in 1600. Creswell got on well with Lord Howard, and initially with the new resident ambassador, Sir Charles Cornwallis (the first for nearly 40 years), but relations soured when Creswell was suspected, with other exiles, of abetting the Gunpowder Plot. Having been upset by Cornwallis' successor, Sir John Digby, who spread rumours that most of the students at the recently founded Madrid college were spies, he retired to spend his last years in Flanders.

During Philip's final years, Jane had not given up hope of going to Flanders, either as Governor of the Low Countries or as leader of the English exiles following the death of Allen in 1594. Allen had petitioned the Pope ten years earlier on Jane's behalf, but the governorship now seemed to be in the hands of the Habsburgs. However, an English Catholic priest had apparently told the Privy Council when arrested that Jane had made 'importunate suit' to Philip to be given the regency of the Netherlands, with her son appointed commander of the army when the Duke of Parma retired. Philip was said to have liked the idea, but it soon emerged that it was a covert plot devised by the untrustworthy Thomas Morgan, with the active encouragement of Jane's self-interested sister Anne Hungerford. At Morgan's urging, Anne wrote to the Spanish Council of State, trying absurdly to convince Philip that not only would it be advantageous for him to have an English Catholic duchess in his dominions so close to England, but that this would cause more 'pain and grief' to Elizabeth than 'any other person of any other nation'. Anne's greater concern, indeed her ambition, was to have more authority within her social circle in Louvain, also access to everyone in Brussels, with her sister as acknowledged leader of the exiles. However, the benefits which would accrue to Morgan, who had plenty of enemies in the Netherlands, were less clear.

Although neither Morgan nor Jane's sister were acting with her interests in the front of their minds, a large part of her longed to move to Flanders and assume the leadership of the English community there. It was her son Lorenzo who intervened and decided what was in her best interests, which was to remain in Spain. The 2nd Duke of Feria's boyhood was spent in religious education, from his mother and his uncle, Bishop of Sigüenza, and in the monastery at Santiago de Ucles, south-east of Madrid, where he served his time as a novice. The experience left its mark when, some years later, he not only completed the building of the convent of Montevirgen at Villalba de los Barros, founded by his parents, but rebuilt and expanded the convent of San Onofre de la Lapa, founded by a previous Count of Feria in the 15th century. This convent, ten miles from Zafra on the road to Portugal, was closed in 1835 and is now in ruins.

In his teenage years, however, the young Duke rebelled against his strict upbringing and led a more colourful life. He was described as '*irreflexivo y licencioso*' (thoughtless and dissolute). At the age of 18 he pledged himself in marriage to the Duke of Najera's daughter, then asked three other aristocratic daughters to marry him. The King ordered him to marry one of them, but Lorenzo refused, claiming it would be against his 'honour', and was placed under house arrest. However, he did marry the daughter of the Marquess of Elche later that year, but she died shortly afterwards. While staying at his castle in Zafra, he got engaged to the Duke of Bejar's daughter, but changed his mind when the Duke of Alba's daughter, Beatriz de Toledo, came along with a promised dowry of 100,000 ducats. Feria was one of the most eligible grandees in Spain, but having married again he continued to maintain his reputation for loose living. A committee of 'moral reformation' was set up by Philip and charged with looking into the behaviour of various nobles during the King's frequent absences from Madrid. The committee described Lorenzo's lifestyle as *depravado* (degenerate) and reported in 1586 that he spent his time in the city's clubs, gambling and consorting with 'ladies of the night'. No doubt Jane intervened with a stern reminder of his duty and the reputation of the family, and Lorenzo soon settled down with a third wife, Isabel de Mendoza, daughter of the Duke of the Infantado. A son and heir was born at the end of 1587, and the following year the family spent time in Zafra, where preliminary plans were made for improving the palace and rebuilding work was begun on the convent at San Onofre. Lorenzo and his mother gave their patronage to a polymath from Flanders—map-maker, archer of the Spanish royal guard, poet and intellectual humanist—called Enrique Cock,* who joined Jane's circle in Madrid and was employed to establish *casas de misericordia* (houses of mercy) there and in Zafra. Lorenzo made generous charitable gifts and looked favourably on the idea of founding a university in Zafra. This was suggested to him by Pedro de Valencia, a distinguished philosopher, historian and royal chronicler who was born in the town.

Lorenzo was back in the King's good books after his third marriage and made ambassador in Rome, followed by Paris where he was urged by Philip to press his daughter Isabel Clara Eugenia's claim to the throne of France (her mother was Elizabeth of Valois). Lorenzo was still in Paris when Henry of Navarre was crowned king and war with Spain continued for another three years. Following his wife's early death while he was in Paris, Lorenzo's next job was Viceroy and Captain General of Catalonia, a position arguably more important than any that his father had held. His main worry was that his mother, under the malign influence of Morgan and with pressure being exerted by his aunt Anne, would be persuaded that she could play a more important role in Flanders than in Spain. As blunt and direct in expressing his opinions as was his father, Lorenzo addressed a lengthy memorandum to the Council of State. He made the point that, in her late 50s, Jane

---

* Cock later settled in one of the Feria estate villages, Corte de Peleas, named Lorenzo as his patron and wrote a poem praising the fertility of the Ferias' land.

Lorenzo Suárez de Figueroa y Dormer, 2nd Duke of Feria.
(Portrait by Daniel Dumonstier, 1602)

deserved a quiet life, which was the very opposite of what she would have to endure from the various factions among the English Catholics in Flanders. She would inevitably be called on to judge disputes between Morgan and his Jesuit enemies. Lorenzo was also concerned at the serious drain on the family's finances which would result from his mother's move. He ridiculed the idea that Jane's arrival in the Netherlands would alarm Elizabeth, nor would it enable his mother to exert her influence over her mostly Protestant relations. In Lorenzo's view the only result would be to make life more difficult for Catholics in England.

Lorenzo openly accused his aunt of only wishing to gain more prestige for herself by bringing Jane to Flanders, and of saying or doing anything to achieve her end. Anne had written to the Bishop of Cassano to accuse those 'ambitious to retain in their own hands the handling of English matters' of trying to stop Jane from going to Flanders, and added that 'little can be done with her son'. But Anne did not go quietly: the following year she lobbied Archduke Albert of Austria, newly appointed Governor of the Netherlands, who wrote to Philip to give his approval to the idea of Jane moving north. Another Armada was being prepared, and Anne may have imagined that her sister could have some role in directing future policy towards England. In any event Lorenzo was able to use his influence at the Spanish court to ensure that his mother stayed put. In a letter congratulating her nephew on his appointment as Viceroy of Sicily, Anne admitted that 'my often troubling you with my rude letters might annoy you'.

During the period of this family quarrel Lorenzo had an important adviser and friend in Thomas Fitzherbert. Early in his life, Fitzherbert elected not to follow his family in the legal profession and was imprisoned briefly for recusancy at the age of 20. Having assisted Edmund Campion and Robert Persons in trying to establish a Jesuit mission in England, he was jailed again before marrying and moving to Paris. Here he actively supported the cause of Mary Queen of Scots, and for a time served as secretary to her former mother-in-law, Catherine de Medici. After his wife died he went on to Spain where he was granted a pension to act as Philip's 'intelligencer' on French affairs. He moved to Rouen for a while and was put in touch with Bernardino de Mendoza, formerly Spanish ambassador in London. A meeting with the Duke of Feria in Paris began a long and fruitful relationship, with Lorenzo treating Fitzherbert as his counsellor and confidant on family matters as well as decisions relating to Lorenzo's career. Fitzherbert acted as secretary to the Council of State in Madrid, succeeding Englefield after he died, and while in Flanders he was rescued by Lorenzo from a false accusation of acting as an agent of Sir Robert Cecil and planning to blow up the magazine at Mechlin. Fitzherbert wrote and published 'an apology... in defence of himself and other Catholykes falsely charged with a fayned conspiracy', which may well have originated with the undesirable Morgan. He was also accused of involvement in another fayned conspiracy, this time against Elizabeth. He was said to have tempted

Edward Squire, formerly employed in the Queen's stables, to poison the pommel of her saddle. No evidence of this unlikely story was found against Fitzherbert, but Squire was arrested and executed in 1598. Fitzherbert did exchange letters and information over several years with William Sterrill, a close friend of Thomas Phelippes.* Sterrill was secretary to the Earl of Worcester, who was praised by Elizabeth as 'a good subject' though 'a stiff papist'. Phelippes had been employed by Walsingham to decipher the coded letters of the Babington plot conspirators, which confirmed Mary Queen of Scots' involvement and led to her execution the following year.

In Madrid Fitzherbert accumulated useful intelligence on English affairs which he passed on not only to Lorenzo but also to his father-in-law, who was a member of the Council of State, to other members of the Council, and to the Spanish envoy at the papal court. While Lorenzo was Viceroy of Catalonia he kept in regular contact with Fitzherbert in Madrid, asking him to keep an eye on his mother and inform him at once if she appeared to be about to leave Spain. Lorenzo was particularly worried by a rumour that Jane might join the suite of the Infanta Isabella and Archduke Albert when they travelled to Flanders after their marriage. However, the family crisis passed, although Jane was still corresponding with Morgan who, according to Lorenzo in a letter to Fitzherbert, made up an absurd story that Elizabeth was moving towards Catholicism. Fitzherbert was highly regarded by Philip III, who increased his pension and provided him with royal lodgings.

At the end of the century Lorenzo was writing frequently to Fitzherbert, from Barcelona and afterwards from Sicily, where he was also appointed Viceroy. In 1601 Fitzherbert was in correspondence with the Earl of Bothwell, nephew of Mary Queen of Scots' third husband. Bothwell had led several uprisings against his cousin James VI and been banished from Scotland. It was an odd liaison: he was in Madrid when he wrote to Fitzherbert, as 'your most loving and affectionate brother'. Bothwell may have been seeking Fitzherbert's support to stop James from becoming king of England, and he appeared to think that the Earl of Mar, then Scottish ambassador in London, had some claim to the English throne. But Fitzherbert was about

---

* Both Sterrill and Phelippes were double agents, working not only for Walsingham, but as important sources for Hugh Owen's espionage network in England they were taking money from both sides.

to leave for Rome to be ordained for the priesthood and was no longer close to political affairs. Bothwell died in poverty in Naples.

Jane, on friendly terms with Fitzherbert, wrote to him on at least three occasions. Her nephew William Dormer, son of her half-brother Robert, was in Rome and Jane asked Fitzherbert if he would 'favour him with your advice and make perfect what yet is raw'. A month later she wrote again to thank him 'most heartily for all the favours you have given my nephew— but I received no letter from him'. She also thanked Fitzherbert for being 'so good and sufficient a friend' to her son Lorenzo, and 'for the good memory you retain of me in your holy sacrifices'. This was November 1606: Lorenzo died the following year and Jane was nearly 70 years old.

Soon after Fitzherbert took holy orders, Jane wrote to him, when a mutual friend was in Rome, to say that she wished her friend well when he went back 'to that godly land of Flanders, where I would I were, but shall never go out of my house'. It was too late for Flanders, but there would be one more opportunity for Jane to leave her adopted country behind.

X

Humble duty to a new king

IN HER SEVENTIETH year, and having reigned for 44 years, Elizabeth was old and getting tired of life. As the historian Helen Castor has put it, the mask of Gloriana was slipping. Her memory and her eyesight were failing, and her periods of depression were more frequent. In the last weeks of her life she spent most of the time lying on cushions on the floor of her chamber. She had never nominated or even acknowledged an heir, but Sir Robert Cecil had been in secret contact with James in Edinburgh to prepare for the succession. At the time of the Armada invasion, James had assured Elizabeth that she had his support as 'your natural son and compatriot of your country'. As a great-grandson of Margaret Tudor (Henry VIII's sister), he was the obvious and only candidate; though it was not until she was on her deathbed that Elizabeth is said to have whispered to Lord Howard of Effingham that her successor should be 'our cousin of Scotland'. The accession of Mary Queen of Scots' son James to the throne of England took place remarkably smoothly. There was 'no tumult, no contradiction, no disorder in the city,' one Londoner noted in his diary; 'every man went about his business, as readily, as peaceably, as securely, as though there had been no change, nor any news ever heard of competitors'.

By the end of the century Jane was no doubt well aware that James was going to get the succession. Her plan, together with Sir Francis Englefield and others, to persuade Philip II that his daughter Isabel must succeed Elizabeth, with the active support of the Pope, had got nowhere. Isabel was governing the Netherlands and Philip was dead. Jane may have recalled that her friend Mary, Queen of Scots, shortly before her execution, had sought to transfer to Philip what she saw as her right to the English throne if James had not become a Catholic by the time that she died. In any event Jane decided to write to James, still the 6th of Scotland, at the beginning of June 1600, in effect to urge him to embrace the Catholic faith. James had sent Lord Sempill as his ambassador to Spain, Jane had become acquainted with him, and it was he who arranged for Jane's letter to be taken to Edinburgh.

It was to an extent typical of a letter addressed to a monarch 'with my humble duty', servile and flattering. But it carried a clear message: as your mother's son, you should follow her religion. She told him of 'the dutiful affection and obligation I had to that blessed queen your majesty's mother, as also of the honour I bear to your majesty... in whom if I might also see her zeal in Catholic religion... And therefore I cease not to beseech daily the Almighty to illuminate your majesty in that behalf, and to make you as great a saint on earth as was your blessed mother, to the advancement of His glory and good of our country.' Jane hoped that James would not think it presumptuous of her to write, but that is exactly what it was. However, the enclosure which came with Jane's letter was even more presumptuous, while her argument, in support of James becoming Catholic, was based on a serious misrepresentation of the facts.

This memorandum, addressed to 'the king's majesty of Scotland', set out 'reasons... whereby it may appear that his best way to obtain the crown of England is to become Catholic, and to give satisfaction thereof to the Catholics of England'. Jane's premise was that there were 'three sorts of men of different profession—the first Catholics, the second heretics, the third of no religion, of which the Catholics exceed in number either of the other, and of the three, the zealous heretics are the fewest, for that the greatest part of all those that live in obedience of the Queen's laws are either dissembling Catholics or men of no religion, which would be as ready to follow a Catholic prince as an heretic, if occasion served'.

'If the king's majesty of Scotland gain the Catholics,' Jane went on, 'he consequently gaineth the greatest part of those that be indifferent or of no religion.' But, she warned, 'if any pretender at home should declare himself Catholic, his majesty of Scotland remaining a Protestant, the said pretender should not only have the assistance of all the Catholics of England but also of all the Catholic princes of Christendom'. In view of James's 'education in heresy' she declared, 'in the state that his majesty now standeth, he cannot make any assured account to have any sufficient party in England'.

More than 40 years had passed since Jane left England, and the great majority of those who practised the true religion during Mary's reign would now be dead. Did she fondly imagine that there were so many 'dissembling Catholics' ready to come out of the Elizabethan closet and declare for a Catholic king? Of the three categories of people listed by Jane, she wrote that 'the zealous heretics are the fewest', which after four decades of a Protestant monarch must surely be classified as fantasy. At the time of Elizabeth's death the population of England was around four million, of which, according to the historian John Bossy, fewer than one per cent were practising Catholics.

Jane's seeming ignorance of the religious position in England cannot really be attributed to her prolonged absence from the country, because she remained in contact with friends and relations both Catholic and Protestant. Can she possibly have thought that her one meeting with James's mother 40 years ago and their subsequent friendly contacts qualified her to advise him to follow in Mary's religious footsteps? Of course Jane would have loved to see Mary on the English throne, but this was past history. It is difficult to see this address to James as anything more than the wishful thinking of an elderly woman (now 62) who remained passionate for the return of her country to the true faith. But there was more than thinking in her long memorandum. There was a determination that James should be made aware of the political advantages of his becoming Catholic. Jane took it upon herself to inform James that the King of Spain would like to 'assist his majesty of Scotland in the attaining of the crown of England, thereby to make and oblige to himself a potent confederate and perpetual friend against France', which as 'so near a neighbour is most dangerous to England'. However, Jane concluded, with the support of English Catholics James should be able to 'overcome his adversaries'.

It may be that James's ambassador in Madrid, Lord Sempill, encouraged Jane to write to the King of Scotland. The previous holder of the title, Sempill's grandfather, had resisted the Protestant Reformation in Scotland and was for a time a supporter of Mary Queen of Scots. However, when the ambassador agreed to dispatch Jane's letter to Edinburgh, he can hardly have expected that she was appointing herself both religious and policy adviser to the King of Scotland. Having known personally six monarchs during her life—Edward VI, Mary Tudor, Elizabeth, Mary Queen of Scots Philip II, Philip III—Jane may have thought she was entitled to express her views to a seventh.

For the next two and a half years James was in touch with Madrid, Rome, Brussels, the English court and, above all, Sir Robert Cecil, but not with Jane. After Elizabeth's death, however, her name was put forward to serve James's wife, the new queen, in the same position of lady-in-waiting that she had held as a teenager at the court of Queen Mary during her marriage to Philip. The plan originated with the papal nuncio in Brussels, Ottavio Frangipani, who thought it a good idea that the Duchess of Feria should move to London and enter the service of Anne of Denmark, who was less than half Jane's age. However, the papal secretary, Cardinal Aldobrandino, thought differently: a Catholic lady-in-waiting from Spain to a queen of England who may have converted to Catholicism was calculated to upset the new king at a time when Anglo-Spanish relations were about to thaw.

There is no record of Jane's reaction to the prospect of returning to England, but she made no mention of it in a second letter she wrote to James in October 1603. Her handwriting and her spelling are difficult to read and interpret—her previous letter must have been penned by another hand— but she addresses Mary's son with great warmth, asking 'your majesty most humbly to have that good conscience of me as no alteration of countries could ever in the least jot alter me towards those of the blood real of my country'. The tone of this letter is quite different from what she had written in 1600. Jane's previous insistence on James becoming a Catholic has been dropped and is not even mentioned. Instead she writes that she has been 'severed from my country and friends and parents most dear to me' by the will of Almighty God, but asks the King 'most humbly while there is life in me to demand and command my services in these parts as liberally as if I lived within the bounds of your majesty's jurisdiction'. This was hardly an offer to come to England to serve the Queen as lady-in-waiting, though in her 1600 letter she had written of Anne's 'rare virtues [which] I highly honour and greatly desire to serve'. No reply to either of Jane's letters has survived.

Although James had in effect repudiated his mother before her execution, he would surely have been pleased to read of Jane's respect and affection for

Mary, and of her recollection of meeting her at Amboise when she was queen of France. If she were still living, Jane wrote, she 'would favour me with her honourable attestation', having in Scotland and in England retained 'always a special memory of me and [made] me participant of her majesty's estate which I always esteemed as a special honour unto me'.* But Jane cannot have done her cause any good in James's eyes by referring to 'my Thomas Morgan' and 'my Morgan' to whom she had entrusted her earlier letters to the King but which had gone astray. Her rather puzzling relationship with Morgan amounted almost to a blind devotion to a man whom no one else trusted. By now he would have received Morgan's extraordinary letter, written a month earlier, in which he had the temerity to advise the King that Jane's half-brother Robert Dormer should be made an earl and to remind him that Jane had done many 'good offices' for his mother in the past.

In her letter Jane did recommend Robert to the King, hoping he would 'make him participant of some part of your majesty's favours in honouring his person and house... in the which I shall receive much joy, seeing in this world I cannot hope to see him'. Her appeal may have touched James because, on payment of a substantial sum, Robert was elevated to the peerage, as Lord Dormer of Wing, in 1615. He prescribed the family motto—*Cio che Dio vuole io voglio*, What God wills, I will—and died the following year. Jane also recommended to the King's favour the Earl of Pembroke;† Viscount Montagu, whose daughter had married Robert Dormer and son had married Mary Dormer; and Lord St John of Bletso, husband of Jane's half-sister Catherine.

Jane's letter to James was written in the last week of October; less than two months later, her sister Anne Hungerford died. 'Her liberality was marvellous, always compassionate... full of good works, imitating the steps of her worthy grandmother,' in the words of Henry Clifford; a tribute which Jane might have struggled to endorse. Thomas Morgan, having failed to find favour with the king of England, his former mistress's son, disappeared from the scene and was not heard of again. Jane may have realised at last that her association with Morgan had done her no good and, if it continued,

---

*   She may be referring to various gifts received by Jane from Mary over the years.

†   Presumably the 3rd earl, whose mother was Mary Sidney, daughter of Jane's uncle, Sir Henry Sidney and herself a distinguished poet, like her brother Philip.

would impede the healing of relations with her son, and might harm any future relationship with the English royal family.

Rumour persisted for another two years. An Englishman at the Spanish court, who was an agent in the service of Sir Robert Cecil, passed on the intelligence that the Duke of Feria's name was being put forward by his mother as Spain's next ambassador in London, in the hope that this would facilitate her appointment as lady-in-waiting.* However, the intelligence was probably faulty: Lorenzo was well aware of his father's unpopularity as ambassador and of the ill-will which he bore Elizabeth. He was equally aware that, with the same bluntness of character as his father, he was not really suited to diplomacy. When he heard that Viscount Montagu had been sent to the Tower for opposing penal laws against Catholics, Lorenzo commented, 'I am very honoured to have such a man as my relative'.

Lord Howard of Effingham, Lord High Admiral, and created Earl of Nottingham at the time of the siege of Cadiz in 1596, pressed the case for Jane to become lady-in-waiting to Queen Anne when he visited the Spanish court in 1605. Having been part of the delegation which had negotiated a peace treaty with Spain in the previous year, Lord Howard came to Valladolid to confirm Philip III's ratification of the treaty. He told the court that Anne was anxious for the Duchess to join her in London, and he would no doubt have renewed his acquaintance with Jane, whom he had not seen for 50 years when he had been one of her suitors. According to Henry Clifford, who was now in Jane's service, Lord Howard told him that his mistress was 'the fairest and sweetest woman of the world; and that the whole court did admire her, and bear her a reverent respect, as well for her own worth as for the esteem the Queen [Mary] did bear her'. Jane may have been tempted by the blandishments of her former boyfriend, but it was too late. She was approaching 70 years old, and her son did his best to discourage the idea, believing that her presence at James's court could only give false hopes to English Catholics.

However, the man responsible for the defeat of the Spanish Armada made a good impression on his hosts during his visit. Having arrived with

---

* The name of Feria continued to attract Cecil's attention. In the same month that Jane wrote to James, the Mayor of Plymouth reported to Cecil that he had arrested an English servant in the Duchess of Feria's employment on his arrival from Spain.

a large staff of officers all dressed in black velvet cloaks, during the negotiations still outstanding he showed by 'his firmness, his calm temper and his unswerving courtesy' that the two countries could be friends again. The newly arrived ambassador in Madrid, Sir Charles Cornwallis, reported that Lord Howard's 'behaviour and his office of admiral hath much graced him with this people, who have heaped all manner of honours that possibly they can upon him. The king of Spain has borne all charges for diet, carriage, etc.' Nor did he leave Spain empty-handed: Philip gave him a diamond and gold feather jewel for his hat, a gold collar set with diamonds, and gifts for his wife and sons. He outlived the king of Spain, and nearly outlived the English king, dying in 1624 at the age of 88. After Jane's son Lorenzo had gone off to be Viceroy of Sicily, his mother never saw him again. He died suddenly outside Rome in 1607, at the same age, 48, as his father had died. He was buried in the chapel, which he had founded, of the convent of Santa Clara in Zafra. (His trusted adviser, Thomas Fitzherbert, joined the Jesuits in Rome, became rector of the English College and died at a great age in 1640.)

Full diplomatic relations between the two countries had been re-established for the first time in nearly 40 years. Jane had known Cornwallis in London in the 1550s when he was comptroller of Queen Mary's household; 50 years on, their friendly relationship was resumed. While Cornwallis was active in attempting to protect English merchants from the Inquisition, he was grateful for advice from Jane, who had had experience of looking after the interests of English merchants in Spain and working for the release of English sailors from prison. Jane was also delighted to be invited to the embassy again. Having served a three-year term, Cornwallis was recalled to London in 1609.

Among Jane's Jesuit friends, Allen and Englefield had died in the last decade of the century and Persons was in Rome, but she still had the companionship of Father Creswell and de Ribadeneyra in Valladolid and Madrid. A Jesuit scholar and professor of philosophy, Richard Gibbons, was writing to her from St Omer in 1602, and two years later, when the Anglo-Spanish treaty had been negotiated, she was in correspondence with two formerly loyal followers of Mary Queen of Scots, Anthony Standen and Thomas Bruce. Standen, as a teenager and page to Mary, had helped her to escape to Dunbar Castle after Riccio's murder in 1566, and was now scheming to get James's wife Anne to come out in support of the Catholic cause. With a similar objective in mind, Jane renewed contact with another of her former suitors from the 1550s. This was Henry Howard, who for years had been under suspicion as a crypto-Catholic, but had kept his head during Elizabeth's reign and immediately made his mark with James, who granted him the earldom of Northampton. He was one of the commissioners who drew up the peace treaty with Spain, for which he was awarded a pension from the Spanish court, and he was appointed Lord Privy Seal, succeeding Sir Robert Cecil. Northampton was also a judge at the trials of Sir Walter Raleigh, Guy Fawkes and the Jesuit priest Henry Garnet. Having supported their convictions, he was described as exhibiting 'a stupendous want of principle'. There is no record of a reply to Jane's letter, which Cornwallis agreed to send from the embassy; and if she hoped her other old Howard boyfriend might give the English king and queen a push in the Catholic direction, she was to be disappointed.

Jane kept up her papal contacts until her last years. Frustratingly, Henry Clifford writes that 'divers Popes have written particular Briefs to the Duchess, commending themselves to her prayers... whose letters I have seen and read'. But he gives no details of the letters, noting only that one was written by Paul V, dated 1st May 1607 from St Mark's, Rome. The Ferias' connections with the papacy were intermittent but continued over many years. On the King's behalf, the 2nd Duke performed the ceremony of obedience to Pope Sixtus V in 1586, to Gregory XIV in 1590 and to Clement VIII in 1592; in 1605 he was received by the new pope, Paul V, on his appointment as Viceroy of Sicily. Jane had received a letter of condolence on the death of her husband from Pius V, and two years later she was granted an indulgence by Gregory XIII. It has been said that she corresponded with four popes, but unfortunately the *Registra Vaticana* end with the pontificate of Pius V, and the Secretariate of Briefs is confused and incomplete.

While papal authority was sacrosanct in Jane's eyes, its inflexible policy towards England sometimes not only put her at odds with Philip but tested her attitude to a military invasion of her country. Because of her undoubted piety and devotion to the Church, she was too easily persuaded to lend her support to an invasion of Ireland which had papal sponsorship. And Pope

Gregory encouraged his nuncios in Spain to make use of what he thought was Jane's influence with her Sidney uncle. Following the failure of the Irish expedition, she became more circumspect in political affairs, and kept her distance from papal policy towards England for the last 30 years of her life.

XI

Back to Zafra

IN THE FIRST years of the 17th century Jane had a new project. Next door to the family's castle in Zafra stands the convent of Santa Marina, founded by her husband's father, who converted it from a hermitage in 1521. By the end of the century, Jane decided that the convent was no longer fit for purpose: the rooms, or cells, were narrow and cramped, the major part would be demolished and a larger convent church would be built. Permission was obtained from the Bishop of Badajoz and Pope Paul V gave his approval, confirmed in a Brief dated November 1606, a year after the works had begun.

Although Jane and Lorenzo bore much of the cost of rebuilding, her first cousin and close friend Margaret Harrington, having no family in Spain, wanted to leave her worldly goods to the convent so that she could be buried in the chapel which was to be built. Margaret had left England with Jane in 1559 and accompanied her to Zafra where she spent much of the next 40 years. Her father was Sir James Harrington who married Lucy Sidney, Jane's mother's sister. Margaret married a *noble caballero*, Don Benito Cisneros, said to be a distinguished member of the Spanish court, and Jane gave her a wedding present of 20,000 ducats. They had two sons, and all three predeceased Margaret. In a will dated January 1601 Margaret provided that she should be buried in the chapel, her body wrapped in the habit of a Franciscan nun, together with the remains of her two sons, who had originally been interred in Madrid. She also gave detailed instructions for her tomb, behind an iron railing, to be surmounted by a statue of her at prayer, kneeling before an altar

The tomb of Margaret Harrington in the convent church of Santa Marina.

with hands clasped. When Margaret died later that year, Jane ensured that her cousin's wishes would be followed and that a tablet on the tomb would bear an inscription, which read, in translation:

'Here lies Doña Margarita Harinton, daughter of Jacobo Harinton, Baron of Exton, and of Doña Lucia daughter of William Sidnei, Viscount de Lisle and Baron of Penshurst, born in England, wife of Don Benito de Cisneros, whose singular virtues could make her illustrious, even though she lacked so many titles of nobility to be so. Pray to God for her. She died in Madrid in 1601. Doña Juana Dormer, Duchess of Feria, cousin, executor and patron of the Church, in fulfilment of her love and of the will, ordered this Chapel and tomb to be built.'*

* After her death, Margaret's brother John was ennobled as Baron Harrington of Exton at the time of James I's coronation and made guardian of his daughter Elizabeth.

When the rebuilding of the church began, Jane gave instructions that a passage should be constructed, leading from the castle to the convent. Now that, thanks to Jane's careful management, the family estate was no longer in debt, her husband's wish that the two buildings should be joined could be fulfilled. The corridor between the two had galleries above and, at the entrance to the church, an oratory for the family when attending Mass. However, the rebuilding and redecoration were not completed until 1609, by which time Lorenzo had died in Italy and his mother had less than three years to live. Today the convent is closed, the church no longer used for worship and the corridor to the castle is sealed. But a plaque on the brick façade of the building records Margaret's name and the *estatua orante de la fundadora* (statue of the founder at prayer). The church, converted into an assembly hall, is now used for occasional cultural events, and on top of the church tower a stork stands contentedly on its nest.

It is remarkable that Jane, aged 67 in 1605 and living in Madrid, should have arranged the rebuilding herself and given the most detailed instructions to the various artisans whom she employed. Through friends and contacts at the royal court, Jane found master-builders, joiners, stone-masons, some of whom had worked on the building of the monastery/palace of the Escorial. Jane knew what she wanted: everything was specified in writing, and it was fortunate that, among all the towns in Extremadura, Zafra was renowned for its skilled building workers, bricklayers and stone-cutters. Jane also chose the altarpieces, sculptures and paintings for the church, commissioning important figures such as the artist Eugenio Cajes, court painter to Philip III, and the sculptor Anton de Morales, both of whom had worked on the famous altarpiece at the monastery of Guadalupe.

There were to be three *retablos*, with the main altarpiece resembling the one designed by Juan de Herrera for the monastery at Yuste, where Charles V died. Jane directed that the paintings and sculptures should include images of Saints Francis, Paul, Lawrence and Anthony of Padua. Her principal joiner, Simon de Peralta, showed her his plans, then went from Madrid to Zafra to assemble the altarpieces, and to repair the damage which some of the artworks inevitably suffered on the 200-mile journey. Much of the work had been completed by 1610, when Jane dictated further instructions in her will for the rebuilding of the choir, cloister and convent dormitory.

Funds were allocated in her will for the completion of the project, but Jane added the proviso that rubble and brick, not stone, should be used where possible, and that the choir-stalls should be plain and inexpensive. Water would have to be piped to the convent. Jane was now in her 70s and in poor health, yet she continued to be absorbed in the details of what she was creating. The final stages of the rebuilding of Santa Marina were begun less than six months after her death. Although she never saw the church and convent which she had planned and designed, it remained as her interpretation of her Catholic faith, and her legacy to the town of her Feria family.

The 3rd Duke of Feria, Gomez Suarez de Figueroa y Cordoba, would have worshipped in the rebuilt Santa Marina and used the passage between the castle and the convent church. He spent time in Zafra after his first marriage, and again during the winter of 1614-15 before he was made Viceroy of Valencia. Born in Guadalajara in 1587, in the palace of his mother's family, the infant Gomez was near enough to Madrid to be taken to see his grandmother on various occasions. Brought up, like his father and grandfather, to serve his king and his God (under Jane's instruction), Gomez also followed his father in his taste for loose women. When Jane learnt that he had been entertaining prostitutes in his coach, she refused ever to step into that coach again. After the death of his first wife, Gomez married a young cousin, daughter of the Marquess of Priego. Following also in his father's more serious footsteps, he served as ambassador in Rome and Paris and, later, as Viceroy of Catalonia. Gomez embarked on a military as well as a diplomatic career and rose to be one of the last able military commanders of the Spanish Empire. He had a reputation for being autocratic and sarcastic, and was known as El Gran Duque de Feria for his exploits in the Thirty Years' War. His outspoken nature also led to confrontations with Philip IV's all-powerful prime minister, Count-Duke of Olivares. As Governor of Milan, Gomez established Spanish garrisons to link Milan with Austria, and in 1633 captured the Swiss city of Rheinfelden, opening direct communication between the Spanish territories of Milan and the Low Countries. A few months later, Gomez died of typhoid in Munich, though it was rumoured that he had been poisoned on the orders of Olivares.

When, many years earlier, he was granted the knighthood and habit of St James, he went to visit his grandmother wearing his red cross on his chest.

According to Henry Clifford's account, Jane spoke to him with these words:

> 'You are now a new man; for in taking this habit, you are entered into
> many obligations; and all are to bind you to be a faithful and valorous
> knight in the service of Almighty God and His Church. This cross upon
> your breast is to put you in remembrance under Whose banner you serve,
> and Whose soldier you are; and so a motive to have Him always before
> your eyes Who by His death made the Cross honourable, as you have it
> for an honour to wear it where you do. And since that His greatest enemy
> is sin, it is your part to fight and war always against sin; for otherwise it
> will be but false dealing to bear His colours and yield to His enemy. Good
> son, reflect upon this, and do your best to put it in practice, and you will
> be honoured both of God and men. And so God Almighty give you the
> joy I wish you with it.'

Gomez then knelt and received Jane's blessing. Unfortunately she did
not live to see how he followed her injunctions, but nor did she survive to
witness the end of the dynasty of Suarez de Figueroa and the Dukes of Feria.
Gomez's son and heir died, aged five, in the same year as his father, and the
title passed to the house of Priego, descended from Jane's mother-in-law, the
Marchioness of Priego, and Gomez's widow.

Gomez's maternal grandmother, the Duchess of the Infantado, called on
Jane one summer's day in 1609 when, apparently taking her arm and twist-
ing it involuntarily, she caused a bone in Jane's arm to break, or splinter, just
above the elbow. Jane was now 71, and no doubt her bones were brittle, but
she was not well served by the doctor, lame and elderly, who was summoned
to repair the damage. She was in great pain, and after Gomez and a physician had arrived at the house, the King's bone-setter was recommended and
called late at night to Jane's bedside. But his resetting of the bone in Jane's
arm also failed to relieve the acute pain, prompting someone to suggest 'a
plain country fellow' from outside the city, who arrived after three days and
did a much better job than the other two. Jane then remained in bed for the
next six weeks, and did not leave the house until October. Her first outing
was to the Dominican convent and church of Our Lady of Atocha, one of
the most important places of devotion in Madrid.

The royal court was now back in Madrid, having moved to Valladolid
for five years, but Jane's contact with Philip III was not nearly so close as it
had been with his father. When Philip's queen (Margaret of Austria) died

in 1611, aged 26 and having given birth to eight children, Jane recorded her condolences in a message to the Queen's Jesuit priest, who had come with her from Austria when, just 14 years old, she married her cousin: 'All Spain and Germany had true cause to mourn; but she was worthy of a better kingdom, which this good lady had attained in so young years; and I, poor woman and decrepit, do languish in this bed with pain and misery.'

This was written in October, less than three months before Jane died. She had not been well since she broke her arm in 1609, and before that she had been showing signs of her advancing years. Her secretary, Henry Clifford, told Jane's half-brother, Sir Robert Dormer, in a letter from Madrid in October 1605: 'I thank God her Grace for her health passeth reasonable well, although troubled often with such infirm and diseaseful accidents as her age is subject unto.' Three years earlier Anne Hungerford had written of her sister Jane's 'recovery from a troublesome sickness that often visited her'.

In January 1609, a few months before Jane broke her arm, Clifford was writing of 'her memory, her discourse, her government, having the management of all her son's estate, the labours that she taketh, rising with the day and presently entering into her oratory, where she remains two hours. Then her chaplain comes to say Mass, which ended, if it be a feast day she goes to church. If not, she disposeth herself to such affairs as are offered.... [She] never goeth to sleep before she hath ended her office and ordinary devotions, which are many.'

When Jane did leave her house, during her final years, it was often to visit a friend who was unwell, when she would take with her a gift of money, wrapped inside a roll of paper. Then, in Clifford's words, 'after salutation and pious advices as occasion was offered, at her coming away, taking leave with words of comfort, [she] would put the paper under the pillow of the sick person'. Others, whether English, Spanish, Irish or French, whom she did not know well, were also in receipt of her bounty, especially those 'of noble blood and ingenuous education, who by some disaster had fallen into wants'. Impoverished English priests were also in the habit of calling at the house to ask for alms and were seldom turned away.

Having assumed the habit of the Third Order of St Francis, Jane tended to be more generous to the Franciscan monasteries in Madrid, to whom she gave bread and eggs, while other monasteries and hospitals received bread from her but had to make do without the eggs. To the Franciscan Poor Clares of the Convent of Las Descalzas Reales (Royal Barefooted), near the Puerta del Sol, she sent supper on Sundays and other holy days. A former palace of Emperor Charles V, this convent was founded by his daughter Juana, Philip II's sister, and the composer Tomas Luis de Victoria spent some years working there. Jane told Henry Clifford that when her country turned back to Catholicism, she would like to be the first to found a monastery of St Francis's Order in England. Instead she left the bulk of her estate to the various monasteries in Extremadura which she and her family had built and restored.

As she approached the last year of her life, Jane concerned herself with certain practical matters. She asked the estate accountant in Extremadura to advise her of all debts and liabilities which had not been discharged, 'so Christian and fervent was her desire completely to satisfy with all that might be due in justice or conscience'. The master carpenter who had supervised the work on the church of Santa Marina was recompensed for having bought more timber than was required—and, at Jane's suggestion, he donated 100 ducats to the monastery. Her servants in Madrid were upset when, a few months before she died, she ordered a coffin to be made and fitted to her body. 'Why weep you? For this must be, and it cannot be long before it come,' Jane told them. 'Weep not, but pray for me. We must all die; but that which imports is to die well and to have a good end. And this is that which I request of you all to commend me to God, that He vouchsafe to give me His grace to end well.'

Jane did have a good end, but until then she suffered a lot of pain, especially in the arm that had been broken, and was confined to bed for most of the year 1611. On one occasion, having held her great-granddaughter in her arms, 'when the nurse took it from her, it so chanced as her arm a little strained, put her to that extremity of pain as she was falling down in a swoon; and after that it put her to such trouble and affliction as she could not lift it to her head, nor pluck out a pin with that hand, but carried it always in a scarf.'

In spite of her sickness, and the pains in her arm and her breast, Jane had a number of visitors, whom her secretary Henry Clifford brought to her bedroom. She always received them, in Clifford's words, 'with that alacrity and cheerfulness of countenance, as increased an affectionate respect from them to her'. Her old friend, the Jesuit father Pedro de Ribadeneyra, came more than once, though he was in his 80s and very frail. She greatly valued his counsel and spiritual support, and when they could no longer meet and talk, they would send notes to one another, carried by Clifford. De Ribadeneyra's last message, which Jane asked Clifford to repeat to her more than once, gave her great consolation: 'Commend me much to the Duchess, and tell her that shortly we shall see each other in Paradise.' He died on 22nd September 1611.

Jane continued to hear Mass every day, and when she was unable to sit up in bed or turn her head, her oratory was moved so that she was facing the altar at the entrance to her chamber. She had her beads, with a death's head fastened to them, and the life of the saint of the day was regularly read to her. When the end was near, according to Clifford's account, she was attended by two Jesuit fathers, four Franciscan friars, one Dominican father and her chaplain. Father Joseph Creswell was one of those Jesuits at Jane's bedside. She had known him for years, since the founding of the English Colleges in Valladolid and Seville, and was grateful for his presence as she lay dying. Creswell had been living at Court in Madrid and having difficult relationships with England's ambassadors, Cornwallis and Digby.

Another visitor was Juan de Idiaquez, now in his 70s, who had known Jane's husband well when he was secretary of state to Philip II, and continued in royal service as state councillor to Philip III, who granted him the title of Duke of Villa Real. Jane spoke of the importance of her faith, of Philip II and life at court, her memories going back to his marriage to Mary Tudor, and of the current Duke of Feria, her 24-year-old grandson. De Idiaquez was much moved when, kneeling at Jane's bedside, he turned to the friars standing behind him and said: 'It is a thing to praise God for, to see this lady how well she stands with God, and the spirit that she hath.'

In the first week of the new year, 1612, Jane began to weaken. One evening, after supper of partridge and jelly, Clifford became very concerned having taken her pulse. The next morning her physicians came and prescribed fresh goat's milk. She preferred to receive the Blessed Sacrament, which was brought to her from the local parish church. That afternoon her grandson came to see her and, on his knees, asked her forgiveness and her blessing. The following day, knowing she had little time left, she asked for the Sacrament of Extreme Unction.

Jane's saintly reputation drew many to her deathbed. Not only her servants now came to say their last, tearful farewells, but a number of *madrileñas*, informed that she was dying, arrived to pay their respects and ask for her blessing. One of her cousins, Sir Robert Chamberlain, was passing through Madrid and came to kiss her hand. (His mother, daughter of John Newdigate, was a sister of Jane's grandmother, Lady Dormer.) 'Cousin, you see my speech begins to fail me,' Jane was able to whisper to him, 'but what I wish is that you stand firm and strong in the Catholic faith. I know well that Catholics suffer great troubles in England; but take care you lose not the goods of heaven for the goods of the earth.' She asked a servant to give him one of her jewels, and sadly he took his leave.

That evening Jane had what Clifford described as 'a trance', probably a stroke or heart attack. She was unable to speak for some minutes, but when she recovered her speech, while holding a small crucifix she recited words from the 6th century hymn *O Gloriosa Domina*. The following morning, the English ambassador's wife, Lady (Beatrice) Digby,* came to the house but left without seeing Jane, who was having another major seizure. But when she understood what had happened, she sent her coach to the embassy, asking Lady Digby to come back. When she returned, she may have been somewhat disconcerted to be warned by Jane, in Clifford's hearing, that 'there is no salvation outside the Roman Catholic Church, nor true faith but that which Catholics profess'. However, one may doubt whether Jane, almost at the point of death, was strong enough to deliver what sounded like a lecture. Lady Digby, who had been brought up in the Protestant religion, apparently replied that she desired nothing so much as the salvation of her soul, and that she trusted that the Lord would have mercy upon her. With that, Lady Digby shed a few tears for Jane's soul and withdrew.

Jane was conscious for a few more hours, lifting her eyes towards heaven and praying to be released finally from her pain and suffering. When asked

---

* After ten years as ambassador to Spain, Sir John Digby was made Earl of Bristol in 1622, but when Prince Charles arrived unexpectedly in Madrid the following year to woo the Infanta Maria Anna, sister of Philip IV, Digby was blamed for the failure of the Spanish Match.

what she wished for, she replied, in English: 'Health in heaven, which I hope will quickly come; for we are in the Vespers of Our Lady of Peace,* who in peace will receive my soul this night. Sweet Jesus, have mercy on me.' Her two great-granddaughters were brought to her bedside for her to bless them, and a short time afterwards she 'rendered her blessed soul to God' and died. When he heard the news, the ambassador Sir John Digby wrote to inform the Earl of Salisbury of her death, describing her as 'the most respected and admired English lady, the Duchess of Feria'.

Jane's body was dressed in a Franciscan habit and a scapular of St Dominic's Order and laid out on a pallet, with her face uncovered and her hands held in prayer. To her devoted secretary, Henry Clifford, her face was 'so beautiful, her hands so fair and flexible, wonderful in that great age, that they seemed rather of a heavenly creature than of a dead body'. The will, which was read to her grandson, consisted principally of bequests to the poor of Madrid and Zafra, and to monasteries in both towns. Masses were prescribed for Jane's soul and for the souls of her husband and son, to be said in various 'privileged altars' in Madrid and in Zafra, where 12 poor men were to be given appropriate clothes to wear in order to accompany her body at the funeral. The Duke was required to sign the will, in which his grandmother gave moral guidance to the new head of the family. He should 'give no place in his soul to sin, nor differ one point from the observances of God's commandments. Be very charitable and an almsgiver; have about thee honest and virtuous company... govern thy vassals with the love of a father... take compassion of the poor, favour the good, repress the wicked and do justice with equality.' It was not the first time that Jane had set out these precepts for her grandson to follow. They may have given him food for thought as he travelled back to Paris to resume his ambassadorial duties.

On the night before she left Madrid, Jane's body lay 'in state' in her house, the coffin surrounded by torches and a black velvet cloth, as visitors came to pay their last respects. The body was wrapped in lead for the journey to Zafra, leaving in a coach before dawn the next morning, accompanied by her chaplain, a friar, family servants and muleteers. In the last week of January the weather was not expected to make the journey easy. Temperatures might be near freezing at night, with storms likely as they skirted the Sierra

* This feast is celebrated on 24th January.

de Gredos. During December, when the weather in Madrid had been miserably wet, Jane remarked to Clifford: 'If I should die now, what trouble should I give my servants to carry my body'. To which he replied: 'Fear not; she that gave not trouble in life will not give it in death'. As if by divine intervention, the weather was fair and almost warm for the duration of 'as pleasant a voyage as could be wished'. The hearse party reached Zafra after nine days, entering the town as it began to rain for the first time in weeks, much to the relief of the locals. The route taken, from Talavera de la Reina via Caceres and Merida, was the same one by which the Ferias had travelled to Zafra in 1560. With a large baggage train, a number of women in Jane's entourage and a son less than a year old, that journey, in the heat of summer, had taken twice as long.

As Jane's body was borne through the streets of her town on the day of Candlemas, the bier passed the family castle, its rounded towers silhouetted against the evening sky, which had now been transformed from Alcázar into Renaissance palace. The coffin came to rest on the other side of the Plaza Corazon de Maria, in the church of Santa Marina, which Jane had built for her cousin Margaret Harrington. The next day, after Mass and a sermon in praise of Jane's good works preached by a Franciscan friar, her coffin was carried with great ceremony, accompanied by priests wearing black velvet copes, the short distance to the convent of Santa Clara. Here it was welcomed by the abbess, Doña Maria de Mendoza, who was related to the young Duke's mother's family. Before the funeral and burial could take place, however, the abbess insisted on satisfying herself that Jane's body was in the coffin. She suspected, with some reason, that the nuns of Santa Marina might have removed the body from its coffin, convinced that Jane should be laid to rest in the church which she had founded.

As one of Jane's executors, Clifford declined to open the coffin. He had the key, the lock had not been broken, and the black velvet covering the coffin had not been disturbed, as all the gilded nails and hinges were in place. But the abbess had heard rumours of what the nuns of Santa Marina were planning, and she was adamant that she must see the body, or there would be no burial. So the coffin was opened and, in Clifford's account

> 'the face seen, which was 12 days after her death, still remaining fair, so
> seemly and sweet and with so lively colours, as if she had been living; her

hands flexible and white as they were while she lived. And out of her nostrils dropped a little blood, so fair, fresh and red, as if it had been from a lamb; which a priest standing there took in his handkerchief.'

After the funeral exequies, which lasted most of the following day, Jane's coffin was carried down to the vault and placed beside that of her husband.

Unfortunately neither of their tombs can be seen today. Until 1770 they lay in the chapel which the 2nd Duke had founded, but were then removed on the orders of the Duke of Medinaceli, who had inherited the Feria title. Lorenzo and his descendants are buried in his chapel, dedicated to a Catalan saint, Raimundo de Peñafort, but only the sepulchre of the 1st Count and Countess of Feria can be seen in the convent church, upright against a wall. The coffins of the 1st Duke and Duchess of Feria were reburied beneath the altar of the church in a vault which was opened for the last time in 1898. No sarcophagus or even a plaque marks Jane's burial place. In her will she apparently directed that her heart should be taken back to England, but it is not known whether her wish was granted. Founded in the 15th century, the convent was intended to be a pantheon of the Feria dynasty, but it lasted no more than 200 years. However, the Franciscan nuns of Santa Clara, or Poor Clares, have remained and today number almost 30. A museum within the convent displays statues and paintings, also relics, some of which were presented to Lorenzo by Pope Clement VIII, and miniature polychrome sculptures commissioned by Jane at the turn of the century. Most impressive is a jewelled cross, formed of precious stones, pearls and rock crystal, which Jane kept in her private chapel in Madrid. At its centre are two wooden fragments representing the True Cross.

Afterword

IN THE 16th century Zafra had a population of some 4,000, contained within a stone wall and a number of gates leading into the town, three of which are standing today. In the various buildings for which the Suarez de Figueroas were responsible over a period of 250 years, and in their patronage of the arts, they benefited greatly from the wealth of talent born and living in Zafra. Francisco and Bartolomé de Montiel, father and son, were both renowned as architects and stone-masons, and they drew up plans for transforming the family castle into a Renaissance palace. Pedro de Valencia, a distinguished philosopher, royal chronicler and humanist, was also involved in ensuring that Jane's meticulous instructions for the Santa Marina church were carried out. The poet Cristobal de Mesa was another *zafrense*: having spent time in Italy with Torquato Tasso and been a friend of Cervantes, he dedicated a long poem to the 3rd Duke and wrote a eulogy to the Feria dynasty when it came to an end.

The dukedom of Feria now passed to the marquessate of Priego (the family of Jane's mother-in-law), and a century later both titles were subsumed into the dukedom of Medinaceli. From 1634 the dukes of Feria have been *duques sin ducado*—dukes without a dukedom—having no connection with Zafra. The current Duke (the 20th), born in 1978, is engaged in the fashion industry in Madrid. His mother was a successful fashion model, Nati Abascal, and his father (the 19th Duke) was sent to prison for kidnapping and corrupting a young girl.

Zafra today, with a population of more than 16,000, has moved outwards from its historic centre, but much of its character remains in the old part of town as created by the Suarez de Figueroa family. Sometimes known as little Seville, Zafra is one of the most charming small towns in Spain. In addition to the Ferias' castle/palace, the churches of La Candelaria and Santa Marina, the convent of Santa Clara, the old Hospital of Santiago, Zafra has

The Feria castle, Zafra, now a parador.

two delightful arcaded squares, the Plaza Grande, and the adjoining Plaza Chica—all within short walking distance. The pity is that the only evidence of Jane's connection with Zafra—she lived there for ten years, managed the Feria estates during her son's and grandson's long absences in Italy, France and Catalonia, built a convent church and was buried in the town—is her name inscribed on the tombstone of her cousin Margaret Harrington.

None of Jane's English family had any connection with Spain, either at the time or subsequently. While the Dormers continued as a Catholic family during the 16th and 17th centuries, their position in the community was respected as holders of the advowson of All Saints Church at Wing. The Dormers' recusancy was passive: they kept themselves out of the lists of recusants in Buckinghamshire and they were never suspected of any treasonable behaviour. As a princess, Elizabeth stayed the night—albeit under house arrest—as a guest of Sir William Dormer, while Jane was at court as one of Queen Mary's confidantes. Robert Dormer, 1st Earl of Carnavon in its first creation, was the grandson of Lord (Robert) Dormer and brought up in the reformed church, but returned to the Catholicism of his family before he was killed at the Battle of Newbury in 1643. The Dormer peerage has continued until the present day, but the family seat, Grove Park in Warwickshire, was demolished in 1976. It had been built by the 1st Lord Dormer in 1615, then replaced by a Victorian pile in the 1830s.

The family of Jane's mother, Mary Sidney, had strong Protestant connections. Mary's brother, Sir Henry Sidney, married the daughter of John Dudley, Duke of Northumberland, who lost his head for having made his daughter-in-law, Lady Jane Grey, a nine-day queen. Robert Dudley, Northumberland's son and Elizabeth's favourite, was the brother of Henry Sidney's wife Mary, and all three were in the Queen's service.*

What is so remarkable about Jane—perhaps because she had family on both sides of the religious divide—is that she made no enemies. During her long life close to the centre of religious and political events in two countries, she was able to form enduring relationships with many of the most significant figures of the 16th century. And in addition to five monarchs—Edward VI, Mary I, Mary Queen of Scots, Elizabeth I and Philip II—whom she knew personally, she also communicated with Philip III, James I and at least three popes.

Her relationship with Elizabeth may not have lasted more than a decade, but it survived the open hostility of her husband towards the Queen. She congratulated Jane on her son's birth, she wrote a friendly letter to her, gently chiding her for not having kept in touch, and she made it clear that if Jane were to return and 'live quietly, she will have my favour'. Elizabeth famously declared that she would not 'make windows into men's souls'; and one of Elizabeth's courtiers said of Jane that 'she was always a kind lady to the Queen'. Yet she never resiled from her Catholic faith and her determination that a Catholic monarchy should be restored in England.

After Feria's death in 1571, Jane became more determined, as she acted as intelligencer to Philip, made contact with militant Jesuit priests and continued to campaign on Mary Queen of Scots' behalf. She communicated with popes, she was stalked by agents of Elizabeth's spymaster Walsingham,

---

* In the next century, Henry Sidney's great-grandson Algernon was a republican political theorist who opposed Charles I and, many years later, was beheaded for plotting against Charles II. During the 1640s both he and his younger brother Robert were lovers of the teenage Lucy Walter, who gave birth to the future Duke of Monmouth in 1649. Charles II accepted him as his son, but so promiscuous was Lucy that it was suggested Robert Sidney might be the father.

yet she maintained good relations with Elizabeth's ambassadors in Madrid. She was a woman on her own, a widow at the age of 33, who for 40 years had to wrestle and juggle with different factions and networks—all in a foreign country where she never came to terms with the heat of summer or the food. Inevitably there were times when she was homesick, not only for England but for Flanders and the English community there.

Jane had demonstrated her strength of character when she decided, against her family's wishes, to marry the Count of Feria. There is no evidence that she regretted her choice of husband, but she must have been embarrassed by his refusal to moderate his opinions on Elizabeth's Protestant regime, or at least to keep his views to himself. He was proud, stubborn, lacking in tact and in understanding of the English people. She respected his integrity and his devotion to the Jesuit cause, and there was no doubting her piety, her charity towards the sick and the poor and what today would be called her social conscience. But one has the impression that she would have welcomed a little gaiety in their marriage. A portrait by Antonis Mor, said to be of Jane but not confirmed, shows a woman of character with a slightly mischievous expression; while the semi-official portrait by Alonso Sanchez Coello, of which there are four versions, has Jane in court dress, looking calm, serious and self-assured. While the Ferias were living for most of the time in Zafra, Jane presided over her retinue of Englishwomen whom she had brought from England. She was in effect continuing the English Catholic court in which she had served under Queen Mary. But it was after her husband's death that she became the doyenne of the English Catholic exiles in Madrid as well as the matriarch of the Feria family and estates.

In her friendship with Elizabeth's ambassadors, and her willingness to help English sailors, of whatever rank, who were arrested for acting against Spanish interests, Jane demonstrated that, regardless of religion, she did not forget her roots; 50 years living in Spain did not diminish her patriotism. The lines from *HMS Pinafore,* which were applied to the spy Guy Burgess in the television drama documentary *An Englishman Abroad,* could be adapted to relate to Jane: 'For in spite of all temptations / To belong to other nations / She remained an Englishwoman.' In her letter to James I on his accession she referred twice to 'mi contre' (my country).

Jane regretted not taking on the leadership of the exiled Catholics in

Flanders which others wanted to thrust upon her, including Persons, who recommended she replace Cardinal Allen in that role after he died. But her continuing association with the sinister Thomas Morgan would have made her life more difficult. Twenty years earlier, after Feria's death, the Pope was in favour of Jane becoming Governor of Flanders, as were Mary Queen of Scots and Allen. It is tempting here to indulge in a bit of counterfactual history. If Feria had lived a few more months, Jane might have succeeded him as Governor of Flanders, as she would already have been in situ. Philip preferred to have her in Madrid as his intelligencer, and was concerned that she would raise her voice on behalf of the Protestant Flemings, but he could have been persuaded to let her stay among the Catholic exiles. Had she done so, whether as Governor or leader of the exiles, and then communicated with either of her cousins, Philip and Robert Sidney, who were Governors of Flushing in the 1580s, might she have had some influence over Philip's decision to launch his armada against England? Jane certainly did not lack courage, and was not afraid of incurring Philip's displeasure. She had witnessed his fanatical drive for Spanish hegemony in the Netherlands, under the Duke of Alba's ruthless policy of repression, and she had made known her disapproval. (Her son's godfather, Archbishop Granvelle, was another to show no clemency towards the Protestant rebels.) Jane was of course aware of the burnings in England ordered by her mistress Queen Mary, of the methods of the Inquisition to stamp out heresy, and of the St Bartholomew's Day massacre in Paris in 1572, instigated by Catherine de Medici, former mother-in-law of Mary Queen of Scots. But, unlike the monarchs and priests who presided over and encouraged these atrocities, Jane did not associate the practice of her faith with the practice of cruelty. Nevertheless, in Jane's eyes they were all the children of God.

Throughout most of her life, Jane was close to the Game of Queens, as Sarah Gristwood's history of the period is titled. Though no queen herself, she was undoubtedly a woman of influence and a saintly figure, deserving of a place alongside the women who made 16th-century Europe.

Family tree of the Dormers and Sidneys

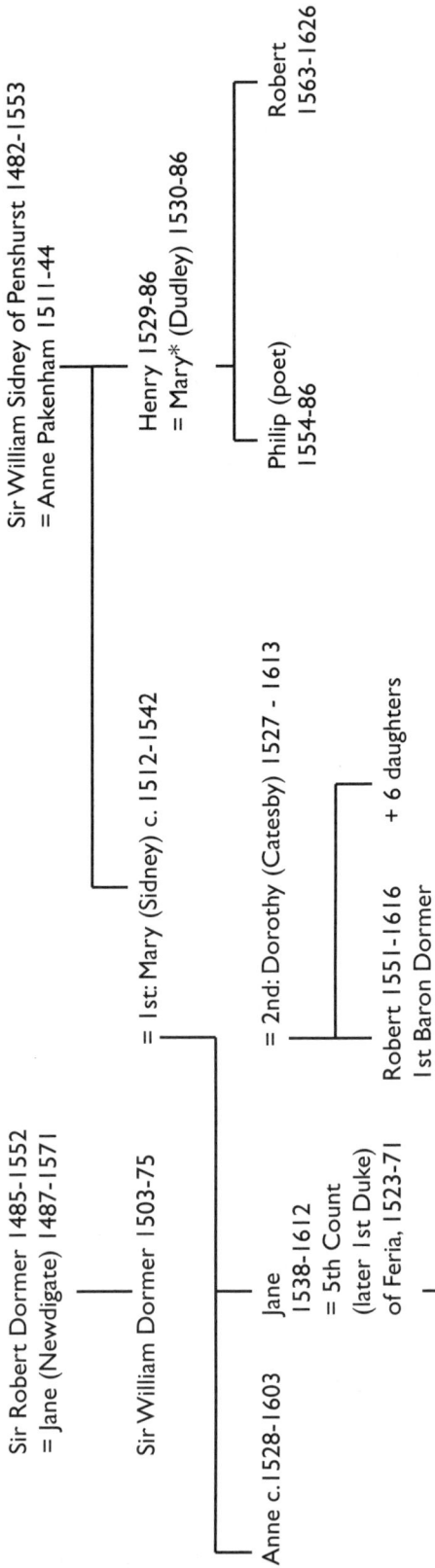

Sir Robert Dormer 1485-1552
= Jane (Newdigate) 1487-1571

Sir William Dormer 1503-75

Sir William Sidney of Penshurst 1482-1553
= Anne Pakenham 1511-44

Henry 1529-86
= Mary* (Dudley) 1530-86

Philip (poet) 1554-86

Robert 1563-1626

= 1st: Mary (Sidney) c. 1512-1542

= 2nd: Dorothy (Catesby) 1527 - 1613

Robert 1551-1616
1st Baron Dormer

+ 6 daughters

Anne c.1528-1603

Jane 1538-1612
= 5th Count
(later 1st Duke)
of Feria, 1523-71

Lorenzo, 2nd Duke
1559-1607
= Isabel de Mendoza

Gomez, 3rd Duke
1587-1634
= Ana Fernandez de Cordoba

* she was the daughter of the
Duke of Northumberland and
sister of Robert, 1st Earl of Leicester

Bibliography

Akkerman and Houben (eds) *The Politics of Female Households: ladies-in-waiting across early modern Europe* (Brill, Boston, 2014)

Alford, Stephen *The Watchers* (Allen Lane, 2012)

Castor, Helen *Elizabeth I* (Allen Lane, 2018)

Childs, Jessie *God's Traitors* (Vintage, 2015)

Clifford, Henry *The Life of Jane Dormer, Duchess of Feria* (Burns and Oates, 1887)

De Lisle, Leanda *The Sisters who would be Queen* (HarperCollins, 2008)

Elliott, J.H. *Imperial Spain 1469-1716* (Edward Arnold, 1963)

Erickson, Carolly *Bloody Mary* (Robson, 1995)

Fraser, Antonia *Mary Queen of Scots* (Weidenfeld & Nicolson, 1969)

Froude, J.A. *The Reign of Mary Tudor* (Continuum, 2009)

Gregory, Philippa *The Queen's Fool* (HarperCollins, 2007)

Gristwood, Sarah *Game of Queens* (Oneworld, 2016)

Howse, Christopher *The Train in Spain* (Bloomsbury, 2013)

Kamen, Henry *Philip of Spain* (Yale, 1998)

Kervyn de Lettenhove, Joseph *Relations Politiques des Pays-Bas et de L'Angleterre Sous le Règne de Philippe II* (Brussels, 1882)

Loades, David *Intrigue and Treason* (Pearson, 2004)

Loomie, Albert J. *The Spanish Elizabethans* (Fordham, New York, 1963)

Neale, J.E. *Queen Elizabeth* (Cape, 1934)

O'Sullivan, Dan *The Reluctant Ambassador* (Amberley, 2016)

Petrie, Sir Charles *Philip II of Spain* (Eyre & Spottiswoode, 1964)

Plaidy, Jean *The Spanish Bridegroom* (Pan, 1970)

Prescott, H.F.M. *Mary Tudor* (Eyre & Spottiswoode, 1952)

Rubio Masa, Juan Carlos *El Mecenazgo Artistico de la Casa Ducal de Feria* (Editora Regional de Extremadura, 2001)

Skidmore, Chris *Edward VI* (Weidenfeld & Nicolson, 2007)

Somerset, Anne *Ladies-in-Waiting* (Phoenix, 1984)

Southern, A.C. *Elizabethan Recusant Prose 1559-1582* (Sands, 1950)

Thomas, Hugh (ed) *Madrid: A Traveller's Companion* (Constable, 1988)

Wiltrout, Ann E. *A Patron and a Playwright in Renaissance Spain* (Tamesis, 1987)

Index